Secrets
East Sus

*Exploring East Sussex with over
twenty-five tours and unusual places to visit.*

Sandy Hernu

S.B. Publications

By the same author:
Exploring Alfriston and the Cuckmere Valley
East Sussex Walks (Brighton, Eastbourne and Lewes)
East Sussex Walks (In and around the rural villages)
East Sussex Walks (Exploring 1066 Country)
West Sussex Walks (Arundel and Worthing)
Secrets of West Sussex

First published in 1996 by S.B. Publications
c/o 19 Grove Road, Seaford, East Sussex BN25 1TP

Revised and reprinted 1998
Revised and reprinted 2003

ISBN 1 85770 097 X

Printed by Antony Rowe Ltd.
Bumpers Farm Industrial Estate, Chippenham, Wiltshire SN14 6LH

Front Cover: Gatehouse, Michelham Priory.
Back Cover: Bluebell Woods, Arlington.
Title Page: Selection of sheep's cheeses
Putlands Farm Shop, Duddleswell.

CONTENTS

INTRODUCTION

There is something for everyone in *Secrets of East Sussex*. This is a book designed to provide ideas for an unusual day out, by introducing the history, the countryside, the trades and the people of East Sussex, both past and present, in an easy to use format. The book is in ten sections, all headed with a descriptive title and a map. In each section are two, three or four tours for the reader to follow, depending on their interests. The tours (indicated on the map) last more or less a day, usually by car. Each place to be visited has the corresponding information, sometimes with a photograph and, if appropriate, a further map contained within the text. For those who do not wish to travel far, there is a 'pick and mix' geographical index.

During the course of researching the material for this book, I became more and more curious by the number of hidden aspects contained in this beautiful county. Most of them won't cost a penny to visit and they are all detailed here, amongst the tours that travel through the following pages. I hope it will give many hours of pleasure, interest ...... and fun.

Alfriston village

LOST VILLAGES

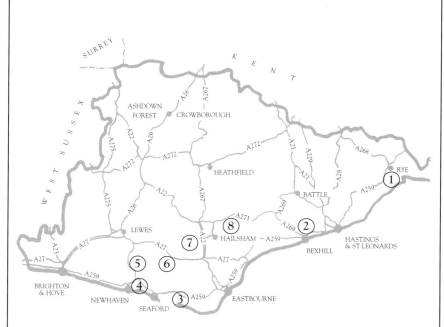

EAST SUSSEX

THE COASTAL TOUR
1. Old Winchelsea
2. Bulverhythe
3. Exceat
4. Tidemills

THE INLAND TOUR
5. Tarring Neville
6. Alciston
7. Sessingham
8. Herstmonceux

Tidemills, from the south, 1883

LOST VILLAGES

The attraction of a ruin, a mere outline or suggestion of a building, always stimulates a hidden curiosity; what happened there and why did it vanish? In John Vigor's excellent book, 'The Lost Villages of Sussex', some thirty odd villages, interestingly all sited in the lower regions of East Sussex, have disappeared since Domesday. Primarily, there were two reasons for this, the Plague and changing circumstances in agriculture. For most, nothing remains, except irregularities of the earth, suggesting some dwellings. This brief history of a handful of the larger 'Lost Villages', will take you to bygone settlements that still have some visible remains and therefore make an interesting visit.

The Coastal Tour

OLD WINCHELSEA (1)

This town has a long and chequered history, dating back to the Saxon era, possibly even earlier. It was destroyed by the raging storms of the 13th century and anything that might have been left lies buried beneath the flat marshland about three miles to the south east of the present Winchelsea. During the 12th century, Old Winchelsea grew to be an exceptionally important port and ship building centre. Its ship's service was noteworthy; supplying more ships and men than Rye, Romney, Hythe, Hastings and even Dover. The population was somewhere between four and five thousand. There were houses, warehouses, inns, mills and churches. It survived ongoing attacks from the French, but the constant struggle with the sea proved

Winchelsea with St. Thomas' church in the background.

6

hopeless. Slowly and surely the land was sinking. By the middle of the 13th century, the port was in dire distress.

The plight of Old Winchelsea was brought to the notice of Edward I. Something had to be done to save it, yet the present site was untenable. Therefore, it had to be evacuated, rebuilt and re-established elsewhere. The King acted generously and gave land from his own manor to the south west of Rye. The new Winchelsea would be built on a hill, similar to Rye and have a large natural harbour to the east. The project was almost completed by the end of the 13th century. Only just in time, for storms, more violent than ever before, hit the old town, breaching the non-existent sea wall and sweeping what was left of the buildings, away for ever. The new town was planned on an ambitious scale. It included thirty-nine squares, the roads criss-crossing at right angles, a town hall, an enormous church and an abbey. But sadly the second Winchelsea did not enjoy its prosperity for long. By the fifteenth century, after constant raids by the French and the Plague, the port began silting up. So, as the sea retreated once more, so did the traders, the ships and its wealth. Today, the town is much smaller, but what remains is very beautiful and almost identical to that laid out six hundred years ago.

BULVERHYTHE (2)

Bulverhythe, long in decay, is now lost amongst the sprawling towns of Bexhill and St Leonards. Yet, once it was a flourishing port, important enough to become a limb of the Cinque Ports in 1229. The name 'Bulverhythe' comes from two Saxon words meaning 'Tradesmen's Harbour'. Today, all that is left are fragments of the Norman chapel of St Mary, built on rising ground behind the ancient Bull Inn.

EXCEAT (3)

The next 'lost village' lies just east of Seaford, at the foot of the Downs after Exceat Bridge. Parking is opposite a complex of barns and Exceat Farmhouse, a restaurant, makes a first class lunch stop. This particularly scenic stretch of coastline, known as The Seven Sisters Country Park, is wonderful for walking and the Visitor Centre, housed in one of the barns, can provide all the necessary information concerning the area. The 11th century village of Exceat, listed in Domesday, was sited on the Downs just above the existing Car Park. Its position near the mouth of the valley, by the River Cuckmere (which was much wider

Site of Exceat church.

then), meant it was convenient for the transportation of goods. Unfortunately, the French also found it easily accessible and carried out several raids. In 1332 the Tax Return shows a population of nearly a hundred. Yet by 1460, Exceat had been depleted and only two houses were left; the rest, including the church, laid in ruins. In 1528 it amalgamated with the neighbouring hamlet of West Dean. Records indicate that the combination of the Plague, attacks from France and ravages by the sea caused the downfall of this medieval village. The site of the church can still be traced and irregularities of the earth could possibly suggest the locations of other dwellings.

TIDEMILLS (4)

Tidemills is sited on level ground between the port of Newhaven and Seaford.. Parking is at the beginning of the track that leads to the remains of the crumbling walls. In the latter part of the 18th century, owing to an increased demand for flour, a large three storey mill was erected on this site for grinding corn. Shortly after, cottages, a blacksmith's shop, a carpenter's shop, even a school sprang up around it. The mill became exceptionally busy, sometimes shifting as much as 1,500 sacks of flour a week. But changes were taking place. The repeal of the Corn Laws in 1846 meant cheaper foreign grain could be imported in vast quantities. In 1853, William Catte, the owner of the mill, died and a savage storm in 1876 caused irreparable damage

Remains of Tidemills.

to all the buildings. In 1884, the mill ceased working and it was finally demolished in 1901. A few families continued to live in this bleak spot, but at the onset of the Second World War, notice was served on the remaining occupants to vacate their premises. Shortly after, Nazi planes screamed across the deserted beach and bombed Newhaven. The destruction of Tidemills was complete.

The Inland Tour

TARRING NEVILLE (5)

Sleepy Tarring Neville is tucked in the lee of low lying downland, on the eastern edge of the Ouse Valley. Listed in Domesday, it claimed to have a population of nine smallholders, eleven villagers and a few workers. This humble farming hamlet, like so many, was devastated by the Plague during the 13th century. Now, a church, a farm and a few cottages are all that remain.

ALCISTON (6)

An attractive village, just off the A 27, sited in a long rambling lane leading to Bo-Peep Hill. The pronounced 'kink' in the road by the little flint church of Norman origin and Alciston Court Farm, marks the dividing line of the northern and southern parts; the latter, except for a couple of cottages, has almost disappeared. During medieval times, Alciston belonged to the monks of Battle Abbey and the splendidly proportioned Tithe Barn, one of the largest in the country, was used to store the 'tithes' or rent, collected from the local farmers. This was normally one tenth of their annual produce. Judging by the size of the barn, the monks were pretty comfortably off; so, when the Black Death struck the community, substantially reducing the population, it was a major blow to their well-being. After the dissolution of the monasteries, the Gages of Firle acquired Alciston.

Tithe Barn, Alciston

SESSINGHAM (7)

A village, mentioned in Domesday when it had a water mill and a population of fifty. Now there is only a farm adjacent to an overgrown site, where the river divides to form a small, naturally moated, island. The track leading from Arlington village towards Sessingham Farm and Arlington Reservoir, was once used by horses and carriages. As late as 1893, surveyors were requested to 'repair the horsebridge at Sessingham'. It is a superb area for walking and an Ordnance Survey map will indicate the many footpaths that meander around the upper reaches of the Cuckmere River. There is also a very good pub at Arlington for those who need extra fortification before an afternoon stroll.

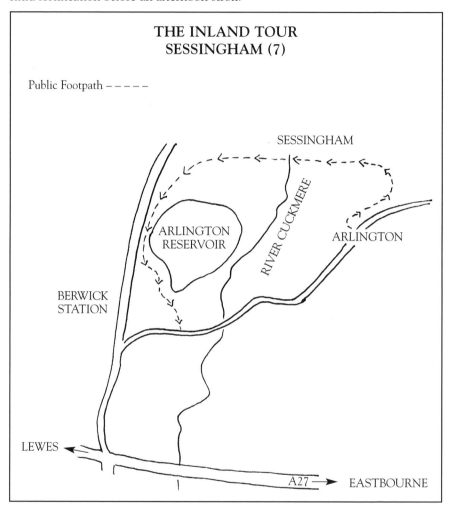

THE INLAND TOUR
SESSINGHAM (7)

Public Footpath — — — — —

SESSINGHAM

RIVER CUCKMERE

ARLINGTON
RESERVOIR

ARLINGTON

BERWICK
STATION

LEWES

A27 → EASTBOURNE

HERSTMONCEUX (8)

Of Saxon origin, Herstmonceux consisted of a Manor and a few homesteads clustered around the church. In those days, the sea reached inland to Herstmonceux, forming the large Pevensey Bay. Today, with sea receded into the distance, the church stands alone, the village now being two miles to the north and the handsome red brick 15th century Herstmonceux Castle sits on the site of the old Manor of 'Herste'. The grounds and attractive gardens are open to the public, but there is an admission charge.

..... OF HISTORICAL INTEREST

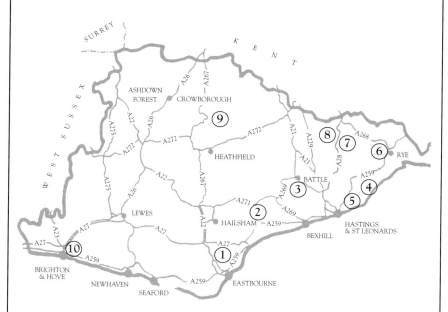

EAST SUSSEX

THE NORMAN TOUR
1. Pevensey Castle
2. Ninfield
3. Battle Abbey
4. Icklesham Church
5. Hastings Castle

THE TUDOR TOUR
6. Rye
7. Queen Elizabeth's Oak- Northiam
8. Great Dixter - Northiam
9. The Middle House - Mayfield

THE GEORGIAN TOUR
10. The Royal Brighton Walk

..... OF HISTORICAL INTEREST

East Sussex, the birthplace of Norman England; it would therefore seem fitting to follow the county's historical progress from that point in time. In this theme, the routes trace the evidence and visit important sites relating to three eras, the Norman, the Tudor and the Georgian. The brief synopsis of each town or place contains information on its architecture, fate and fortunes, as well as something about the famous who influenced the heritage we see today.

The Norman Tour

PEVENSEY CASTLE (1)

Visit the place where the Norman army, led by William the Conqueror, landed on that famous date, 1066 - indelibly printed on our minds since schooldays. It's almost impossible to imagine this peaceful spot awash with some fourteen thousand soldiers. The coastline looked very different then. The neglected Roman fort of Anderida stood in isolation on the Pevensey peninsula and the sea swept back to Hailsham. It formed a large, shallow harbour reaching to Bexhill. Today, this is all marshland and an invasion of sheep has replaced the invading army of 1066.

At the Norman Conquest, Pevensey was granted to the Conqueror's half-brother, the Count of Mortain. It was he who built the moated Pevensey Castle within the walls of the old fort of Anderida. Besieged many times, it has housed some illustrious prisoners, including James of Scotland in 1314. Pevensey Castle lies

North and East towers, Pevensey Castle.

about four miles east of Eastbourne and there is an admission charge to visit. However, the grounds outside the castle walls, yet within the walls of Anderida, are free and well worth exploring. On the western edge is the Church of St. Mary, Westham, supposed to be the first church the Normans built. The intriguing Mint House, opposite the car park by the castle, is over six hundred years old and erected on the site of a Norman mint.

NINFIELD (2)

After leaving Pevensey and turning along the B2095 to Battle, you will pass through Ninfield. It's almost impossible to imagine this rather suburban village once being the site of the Victory Banner, hoisted by the Conqueror, after winning the battle of Hastings. The solid iron Stocks and Whipping Post, set on a triangle of green by the turning to the church, are regrettably not of the Norman era; but they are 17th century and cast in a local Sussex foundry.

BATTLE ABBEY (3)

Somebody once wrote (and I can't remember who), that Battle is where England first realized, "it had woken up with a Saxon kingdom and gone to bed with a Norman one".

The Battle of Hastings was fought on the hilly slopes surrounding the Abbey, founded by the Conqueror in thanksgiving for his victory. By tradition, the high altar of the church marks the spot where King Harold fell. Little is left of the

The Abbey gatehouse, which dates from the early 14th century. The photograph has been taken inside the grounds.

Norman structure. Unfortunately, the church, chapter house and part of the cloisters were destroyed when Henry VIII granted the Abbey to Sir Anthony Browne after the dissolution of the monasteries in 1538. The Abbey and the magnificent gatehouse, built in weathered sandstone, are open throughout the year and there is a charge. Inside the gatehouse, graphic tableaux and information re-create the events of 1066. The Abbot's house, which has been subject to alterations, is now a school.

ICKLESHAM CHURCH (4)

Yet another church claiming to be the first the Normans built. When the Conqueror landed, he seized the Hastings peninsula. This encompassed all the high ground east of Pevensey Harbour, finishing at the Brede estuary. Many churches were quickly established, often on the sites of destroyed Saxon ones. The attractive All Saints Church still has some fine Norman features, especially the large pillars and arches in the nave. Icklesham is situated on the A259 road, Hastings to Rye. Opposite the church, down a small lane, is the Queen's Head pub. As well as some fabulous views from the gardens, it makes a good lunch stop before visiting Hastings Castle.

HASTINGS CASTLE (5)

In a commanding position, atop a high wedge of ground overlooking the sea, are the ruins of Hastings Castle. In its heyday it covered eleven acres, but now it is a mere shadow of its former self. Initially, in 1066 a Motte and Bailey type structure was

Hastings Castle.

erected. However, the Conqueror grew to like his important hilltop castle that guarded the route to Normandy and the rebuilding of a much grander edifice in stone, soon commenced. Hastings thrived for about two hundred years, then disaster struck in a series of violent storms. Untold damage was done, including a large part of the cliff falling into the sea; plus a substantial portion of the castle. The plundering and burning inflicted by the French in the 14th century did little to help Hastings' dwindling fortunes and slowly it declined into being an obscure fishing village. The Castle fell into ruin and remained derelict for more than three hundred and fifty years. During the mid 19th century, the crumbling walls were excavated and restored and made something of a tourist attraction. Hastings became a fashionable resort once more. Rather sadly, two sections of the Castle grounds were removed at that time, to make way for the handsome properties of Pelham Crescent and Wellington Square. The Castle is open all year and there is an entrance charge. A convenient cafe, with a vista across the seascape, is close to the Castle walls.

The Tudor Tour

RYE (6)

No visitor can fail to enjoy Rye: it still retains all the atmosphere of a medieval fortified town and in a flash, one is transported back to the Elizabethan era. The cobbled streets and period architecture are sheer delight to the artist, who frequently captures on canvas, the famous Mermaid Street rising steeply from Strand Quay. Sporting the sign of a wishful sea-maiden, is the heavily beamed Mermaid Inn, rebuilt in the 15th century. Nearby is the house that belonged to Samuel Jeakes, author and astrologer. The Landgate, once part of the old town

St Mary's Church, Rye.

wall, provided the only access to Rye when it was surrounded on three sides by the sea. The rather grim 13th century fortress, Ypres Tower, is now a museum; whilst the splendid church of St. Mary sits astride the summit of this low hill town. The tower has one of the oldest working church clocks in England and the gilded 'quarter-boys' strike every fifteen minutes. Inside the entrance to the church, the long gilt pendulum swings slowly above our heads. Tradition suggests this clock could have been a gift from Queen Elizabeth I, who visited Rye in 1573. She had a great liking for the town and affectionately christened it 'Rye Royal'.

So, what was Rye like in Tudor times? When Henry VIII came to the throne in 1509, it was probably reaching the peak of its prosperity. The population was around 5,000; it had recovered from the plundering and burning of the 14th century raids from France; it commanded one of the best harbours in the south-east and could provide shelter for up to 400 ships. The town was inhabited by wealthy merchants who owned substantial houses around the church, Mermaid Street and Watchbell Street. Fishing and commerce were the main things that contributed to Rye's wealth and during her Tudor prime, fishermen formed half of the population. At the end of the 16th century, Rye's fortunes started to deteriorate. Alarmingly the harbour started to silt up and it could no longer cater for so many ships: therefore, the wealthy merchants commenced trading elsewhere. The fishing industry declined and suddenly Rye was no longer a major English port.

Today, the sea has receded some two miles and we are left with a river and a historically beautiful town, whose only misfortune is to, understandably, attract too many tourists. But go and explore it on a wet and windy day, then the narrow streets will be empty and the ghosts of the past will be yours alone.

The Mermaid, Rye. (Claims to be the oldest haunted inn in the country.)

QUEEN ELIZABETH'S OAK - NORTHIAM (7)

All that remains of a huge spreading oak tree is the stunted trunk, kept together by chains. In 1573, Queen Elizabeth I chose to sit under its spreading branches, eat a meal and for some odd reason, change her shoes, before continuing to Rye. She left behind the green damask pair she was wearing and these are on display at the nearby Brickwall House. The oak is sited on the village green in Northiam.

GREAT DIXTER - NORTHIAM (8)

Great Dixter is probably one of the best surviving examples of a Tudor Hall House. In a Hall House, the main living area was open to the rafters and usually had a central fireplace. Dixter was no exception: the Great Hall measures 41 feet by 26 feet and 31 feet high. The massive timbers, taken from the local Wealden forests, once had to support a Horsham stone roof as well as the fireplace; it is still possible to see where the timbers have been blackened by smoke.

When Mr. Nathaniel Lloyd purchased Dixter in 1910, it was actually two separate and derelict Hall Houses, Benenden and Dixter. Under the guidance of Sir Edwin Lutyens, they were sensitively restored and joined together by the addition of a wing. Both the house and gardens are open from April to October and there is an admission charge. It is well signed from the A28 at Northiam.

Great Dixter, Northiam

THE MIDDLE HOUSE - MAYFIELD (9)

An elaborately timbered house, built about 1575 and probably one of the finest Elizabethan buildings remaining in England. One of its early owners was Thomas Houghton, Principal of Cliffords Inn in London. Middle House became an inn in the mid 1920's and remains so today. Do go inside, if only for a drink; it's worth it, just to see the heavily beamed and carved interior. Much of the property in Mayfield has medieval origins although most have been altered to accommodate shops. It is a pleasant, if somewhat busy village, but well worth visiting. Near the centre of the High Street are the remains of the 14th century Archbishop's Palace, now incorporated into the more recent structure of a school.

THE GEORGIAN TOUR
THE ROYAL BRIGHTON WALK

The Georgian Tour

THE ROYAL BRIGHTON WALK (10)

The Georgian era covers the reigns of the first four Georges, 1714 - 1830. Included in the latter years was the Regency style favoured by The Prince Regent, later George IV. There is nowhere better equipped than Brighton to offer an architectural insight into those elegant buildings of the early 19th century.

Most are well versed with the basically true story of The Prince Regent coming to Brighton to partake in sea bathing: a cure for all ills. He subsequently fell in love with the place and to suit his extravagant needs, had a simple farmhouse converted into the Royal Pavilion. So, fashionable Brighton began, but it did have a history before Prinny, as he was affectionately known, arrived. It started life as a fishing village and rose to being the second largest town in Sussex, the economy still based on fishing. The town, as it stood then, was more or less encircled by West Street, North Street and East Street. Castle Square, where the Pavilion is sited and now appears to be the hub of Brighton, then lay on the corner of the old town. This was how the Prince Regent found it. The oriental conversion of his rustic farmhouse needed considerable imagination and a lot of assistance. In fact it took several stages and thirty odd years.

The original farmhouse was refurbished in a classical style by Henry Holland in 1786. Initially, it was known as the Marine Pavilion of His Royal Highness. In 1802 it was enlarged and given a Chinese interior. Then came an impressive separate addition of a Hindu style riding house and stables; today known as The

Entrance to the Royal Pavilion, Brighton.

19

Dome and The Corn Exchange. Finally, in 1815, the conversion 'extraordinaire' started on the Pavilion, under the guidance of the famous architect, John Nash. His work has remained almost unaltered and that is what we see today. So it seems appropriate to start exploring Georgian Brighton on foot from this landmark.

I think one should allow half a day for visiting the Royal Pavilion and the immediate surroundings. Probably it is better not to give any directions but simply to wander leisurely amongst this oasis of historical extravaganza. Just south of the Pavilion (having crossed the road) is Steyne House, now the YMCA. This was built in 1804 for Maria Fitzherbert, the Prince's favourite mistress, who eventually became his wife. The property, although still handsome, has sadly been much altered. Do ensure a look at the Dome and the Corn Exchange. Housed in these buildings is a first class museum and art gallery; much of it gives an insight into Brighton's past and what's more it's free. There is also a rather quaint galleried coffee shop in the museum. It overlooks the Art Nouveau room and provides a welcome refreshment stop before moving on to the lesser known Kemp Town.

The building of Kemp Town, named after its developer, Thomas Read Kemp, started about 1800. The original Kemp Town was sited around Sussex Square and Lewes Crescent; today it has grown to encompass a great deal more. The walk travels along Marine Parade, the seafront road east of the Palace Pier, for a mile and a half. It investigates some of the finest squares and terraces in Brighton and also the famous names associated with them.

a. From the Pavilion walk to Marine Parade, by the Aquarium and Palace Pier. Notice Camelford Street, with its charming rows of fishermen's cottages.

b. On the corner of Rock Gardens is a property with a particularly unusual hooded balcony.

c. Do walk to the top of Bedford Street and visit St. John the Baptist Church, almost opposite in Bristol Road. Mrs. Fitzherbert is buried here and her effigy shows her in the kneeling position wearing three wedding rings: one for each of her marriages, including that to George IV.

d. Royal Crescent, built about 1800 by J. B. Otto, a West Indian speculator. It is not known who designed this stunning crescent, but the exterior is unusual. All the properties have been fronted with black mathematical tiles, which seemed to become a feature of Georgian Brighton. Perhaps they were used because tiles were less prone to corrosion by the salty air than bricks; or maybe it was to avoid the Brick Tax that was in existence around that time.

e. Narrow Bloomsbury Street has identical rows of beautifully proportioned houses that are finally being restored.

f. The stuccoed Marine Square was erected about 1824 and laid out by the local influential solicitor, Thomas Attree. The facades are plain, yet gracious and pleasing in their simplicity.

g. Portland Place was designed by Charles Augustus Busby: the drawings for it were exhibited at the Royal Academy in 1830 and it was to be his final work in Brighton. The nearby church of St. George is also attributed to him.

h. The formal L-shaped Eastern Terrace has, for some reason, had the addition of extra balconies. Note the property at No.1; the walls are so curved that the internal rooms resemble those of a windmill, being almost circular. It has seen some famous faces. Albert Sassoon lived here for twenty years, between 1876 and 1896. He entertained the Shah of Persia in 1889. Edward, Prince of Wales lunched with him in 1881 and again in 1896, five years before his Coronation in 1901.

i. Belgrave Place and Eaton Place were both erected by the renowned builder, Thomas Cubitt in the mid 18th century.

j. The impressive Lewes Crescent and Sussex Square, the latter leading off from the former, are the pearls in the oyster. These, together with the terraces that flank them, comprise the main estate of the original Kemp Town. The entirety had a variety of different builders and architects, but work was initially started about 1823.

k. Finally, step across the road from the Georgian era to the 20th century. From here there is an excellent view of Brighton Marina. Apart from every conceivable form of modern sailing boat, it has a good selection of shops and restaurants.

Royal Crescent, Kemp Town.

INDUSTRIAL SUSSEX

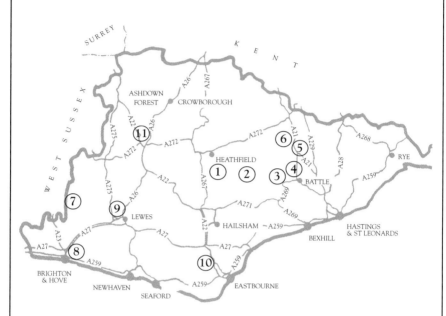

EAST SUSSEX

THE IRON TOUR
1. Warbleton
2. Dallington
3. Ashburnham Forge
4. Penhurst
5. Sedlescombe
6. Ripley's Forge & Museum
   of Rural Life - Robertsbridge

THE WINDMILL TOUR
7. Jack and Jill - Clayton
8. Rottingdean Mill
9. The Round House,
9. Pipe Passage - Lewes
10. Polegate Windmill
11. Nutley Windmill

INDUSTRIAL SUSSEX

It's almost impossible to envisage East Sussex as the industrial heart of England; yet during the 16th and 17th centuries, when iron smelting was at its height, that is exactly what it was. Iron had been worked in various parts of the Weald since Roman times and the method changed little over the years until the end of the 15th century, when demand increased substantially. A more sophisticated operation, initiated from Europe, was then put into practise: huge stone lined furnaces sprang up, with large water-operated bellows working night and day. Shacks were erected around the forges to house the workers. Streams were dammed, making hammer ponds to provide power for operating the machinery and thousands and thousands of trees were felled to feed the insatiable fires. The foundries produced everything from canons or stocks, to pots and pans. It was not until the 18th century that demand subsided in this area. Coal had been discovered in the Midlands and it was cheaper to burn than charcoal, so the foundries gradually moved north, where the mining of coal took place. This tour visits some key iron working sites and travels through the beautiful landscape that once was an ugly barren wilderness, scarred from overuse.

The Windmill Tour should perhaps be called the 'Sunday Tour', for it seems to be the only day the mills are open and if you're lucky, in operation. Historically, of course, water mills are older but a type of windmill has been around in this country since the 12th century. Yet it was not until the late 18th century, when there was a marked increase in the amount of land being used for arable purposes, that Sussex saw it tides of prosperity change once more and the miller and his windmill went into serious production. In this county alone there were over a hundred windmills. Within two miles of Brighton there were eight: Hastings had sixteen and Lewes was adorned by the sweeps, towers and smocks of many windmills. Sadly, most have fallen into decay and disappeared, or converted into some odd truncated dwelling. Just a few windmills remain and these have fortunately been preserved so that we can still get some idea of our industrial heritage.

From the archives come these two gems: "1797. A miller in Brighton, with many onlookers, moved his entire mill with a yoke of 36 oxen and a lot of men, more than one mile without the slightest accident."

"By what fair air I grind ye grain, Make good prayer when bread ye gain."

The Iron Tour

WARBLETON (1)

Richard Woodman, known as the 'Iron Man of Sussex', found fame and wealth in his early twenties. He lived in Warbleton, owned two furnaces, a busy forge and employed a hundred people. Unfortunately, religion proved to be his downfall. He refused to accept England's return to Catholicism under the fanatical Queen Mary I and when his beliefs became public knowledge, he was arrested and imprisoned in the church tower at Warbleton. In 1557, at the age of thirty, he was burned at the stake in Lewes.

The attractive village of Warbleton, lies a few miles south east of Heathfield and boasts an extremely good pub called the 'Warbill-in-Tun'. It dates from the 17th century and the strange name, which sounds like a play on Warbleton, was supposedly acquired during the Civil War when soldiers tried to open a barrel, or tun of beer, with an axe.

DALLINGTON (2)

Situated just off the B2096 road to Battle, is the charming hamlet of Dallington. Positioned on one of the highest points of the Wealden ridge is the church which, undoubtedly has the best and most extensive views across the old iron working landscape. There is little evidence of it today. Gone are the chimneys, the smoke, the workers, the dirt and the activity. However, a glance at an Ordnance Survey map will show the sites of many of the old ironworks and reveal names such as, Furnace Lane, Hammer Wood, Iron Brook, Forge Bridge; all an indication of a long gone industry. In the churchyard at Dallington are some very interesting, if rusty, examples of local iron, used for surrounding gravestones.

Ironwork, Dallington churchyard.

ASHBURNHAM FORGE (3)

Finally closing in 1820, Ashburnham was the last working foundry in East Sussex. The forge, now converted, is a part of the Ashburnham estate and sited by a weir in the wooded valley, through which the Ash Bourne stream flows. Ashburnham is set deep in the countryside and to get there, one must take a turning to the north from the B2204 Battle road, then using minor roads, follow the signs. A few hundred yards east of the forge is a public bridlepath leading up the tree-lined valley. This is the site of the two large and busy Ashburnham ironworks. Today, it makes a very pleasant walk, especially if one can catch a glimpse of the wild deer that inhabit the area.

PENHURST (4)

Once seen, never forgotten. Penhurst has been described as a 'rare and exquisite manorial group', stunning in both simplicity and setting. Positioned on high ground, about a mile east of Ashburnham, is the 16th century iron master's manor, with a church of a similar era and a complex of ancient barns; that is all. It rests undisturbed by the 20th century.

SEDLESCOMBE (5)

A pleasant village, a mile or so from the A21 and built on sloping ground by the River Brede. In the 17th century the river was navigable up to Sedlescombe. Barges would moor against the banks, fill up with a cargo of iron, then return to Rye where it would be shipped to London. Today, the river is a peaceful trickle and it seems odd to think, only three hundred years ago it was a hub of ceaseless activity. A mile and a half east of Sedlescombe, along Brede Lane, Powdermill Reservoir marks the site of the old Brede furnace. Richard Leonard, master craftsman, worked there and became famous for his fire backs. One of these can be seen on the outer walls of Bridge Garage in Sedlescombe.

RIPLEY'S FORGE AND MUSEUM OF RURAL LIFE. ROBERTSBRIDGE (6)

What better way to end the foray into the history of iron, than to visit a present day working forge reproducing fire backs, firedogs and baskets, similar to those used during the 16th and 17th centuries. The long low buildings that accommodate the forge, showroom and museum, are sited at the northern end of Robertsbridge, opposite a car park.

The Museum of Rural Life reincarnates long gone local businesses, such as "Jack Hook's Smithy", "Mr. Beaney's, Wheelwrights", "Jim Beedon's, Cobblers", "Farming Bygones" and others. All the artefacts are local and amongst the vast array are some splendid and genuine examples of iron crafted during the industrial era. The Museum is open every day, except for Christmas, when it is closed for one week. Whilst here, do have a look around the quaint village of Robertsbridge. It's near the A21 road, about eight miles from Hastings and the local pub makes a very pleasant stop.

Museum of Rural Life, Robertsbridge

The Windmill Tour

JACK AND JILL, CLAYTON (7)

Above the village of Clayton, a few miles north of Brighton, are the husband and wife windmills, Jack and Jill. Side by side, they are importantly placed on a high stretch of downland, having some wonderfully scenic walks surrounding them. Jack is a black Tower Mill; built in 1866, he was worked until 1906 and is now in private ownership. Jill is a white Post Mill; built in Brighton about 1821, she was later transported by a team of eighty oxen to her present site in 1852. Like Jack, she ceased milling in 1906, but in recent years has been completely restored and is open to the public on Sunday afternoons.

ROTTINGDEAN MILL (8)

Erected in 1802, Rottingdean Smock Mill is positioned on Beacon Hill, west of Rottingdean village. For eighty years it kept the local inhabitants supplied with flour. It also played an important part in smuggling, with the cellars being handy for storage and the sails being turned to signal to boats lying offshore. Supposedly, this tarred windmill is the one used by Heinemann, the publishing house, on the spines and title pages of their books. Like other windmills, the changes in agriculture caused it to become empty and dilapidated; even the large flocks of sheep that grazed beneath the sails, disappeared to make way for a golf course. Fortunately, the mill has now been the subject of major refurbishment and those wishing to visit should get in touch with the Rottingdean Preservation Society, via the Grange Museum in Rottingdean (see Literary Sussex).

THE ROUND HOUSE, PIPE PASSAGE, LEWES (9)

To the western foot of Lewes Castle precincts is Pipe Passage; the curious name being acquired from the clay pipe making business, which operated there during the early part of the nineteenth century. The Round House, sited at the top of the Passage, is the converted base of a windmill built in 1802. It did not remain there for long; by 1853 the working section had been dismantled and re-erected at Race Hill, on the outskirts of Lewes. About 1919, records seem to conflict as to the exact date, Virginia Woolf saw, fell in love with and purchased The Round House for £300. It was an impulsive decision, obviously later regretted, for after a few weeks it was put back on the market again and the Woolfs bought Monks House in Rodmell (see Literary Sussex).

This area of Lewes Old Town is particularly picturesque, so do look around it. Opposite Pipe Passage is Bull House, where Tom Paine of 'Rights of Man' fame, lodged. Beyond, is the steep, cobbled Keere Street. A little further on, past the large Georgian fronted houses, is Shelley's Hotel, built in 1577 and home to the Shelley family for many years.

POLEGATE WINDMILL (10)

Polegate Windmill is near the A22, four miles north of Eastbourne. It is the only Tower Mill open to the public in East Sussex. This particular type of mill has the entire 'cap' turning by means of a fantail set at right angles to the main sail. It was erected in 1817 and continued milling, almost constantly, until the early 1960's when, due to the retirement of the miller, it came up for sale. Planning permission was then sought to demolish the building and develop the site for housing. Eastbourne Civic Society intervened and purchased the mill for preservation as an industrial monument in 1965. After extensive

Interior of Polegate Windmill.

restoration, Polegate Windmill, together with a small milling museum, was opened by His Grace The Duke of Devonshire in 1967. It continues to be open every Sunday from Easter until the end of October and there is a very small entrance fee.

NUTLEY WINDMILL (11)

Amongst the purple heathland of Ashdown Forest is a superb example of a late 17th century, Open Trestle Post Mill. It is one of the oldest mills in Sussex and one of the five remaining Post Mills in England. However, the history of Nutley Windmill is a little difficult to trace. It has been dated as being somewhere between 1680 and 1730, yet there is no evidence of it being on its present site until 1836. So, where did the mill get to during that hundred odd years unaccounted for? Presumably it was moved from another site, which was not an uncommon occurrence. Yet there is no record of it being on another site within a reasonable distance. The mystery still remains unanswered.

So, why is it called a Post Mill? In a Post Mill the entire structure containing the machinery and millstones pivots to face the wind on a central 'post', usually the massive trunk of an oak tree. This is steadied by four quarter bars, mortised into the post at one end and let into a pair of cross trees at the other. This design has been known since the 12th century and all earlier windmills were built like this.

Nutley Mill is near the A22, north of Nutley. Restored to full working order during the seventies, it is now open on the last Sunday of every month throughout the season and there is a small charge.

FOLLY SPOTTING

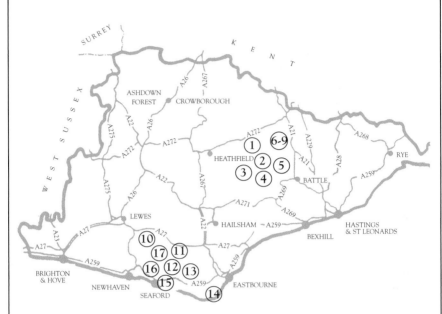

EAST SUSSEX

'MAD JACK' FULLER'S TOUR
1. The Brightling Needle or Obelisk
2. The Observatory - Brightling
3. The Sugar Loaf - Woods Corner
4. The Rotunda Temple - Brightling Park
5. The Tower - Brightling
6. Rose Hill - Brightling
7. The Pyramid
8. Brightling Church
9. The Estate Wall

THE SOUTHDOWNS TOUR
10. The Gamekeeper's Tower - Firle
11. The Long Man - Wilmington
12. Lullington Church
13. The White Horse - Litlington
14. Belle Tout - near Eastbourne
15. Martello Tower - Seaford
16. Market Cross - Alfriston
17. The Flint Tower - Alfriston

FOLLY SPOTTING

What is a Folly? The dictionary states: "an extravagant and useless structure." Alternatively, what about a structure built for a particular use that has now become redundant; could this not take on the guise of a folly thereafter? In this theme there is some of each.

The first tour takes place in Brightling, four miles west of the A21 at Robertsbridge. It investigates the wealthy eccentric, John Fuller who, on account of his folly building, was known as 'Mad Jack'. Born in 1757, he had, by the age of twenty, inherited the family estate, Rose Hill in Brightling. He represented Sussex in four Parliaments, where his ebullient personality and twenty-two stone frame gave rise to all sorts of risqué stories. He was, nevertheless, a good and generous man and when he left the political scene in 1810, concentrated on local welfare, arts and science and of course, folly building.

The second tour hugs the scenic downland that lies near the coast between Lewes and Eastbourne. Here the follies include not only unusual constructions, but hill carvings, a tiny church, a cross and a lighthouse. They all have a tale to tell.

'Mad Jack ' Fuller's Tour

THE BRIGHTLING NEEDLE OR OBELISK (1)

A sixty-five foot obelisk standing atop Brightling Beacon, marks one of the highest points in Sussex. Constructed of stone blocks, it is thought to have been erected to celebrate Wellington's victory over Napoleon in 1815. This prominent landmark is situated on private land, but it can easily be seen from the road a mile west of Brightling.

The Brightling Needle.

THE OBSERVATORY, BRIGHTLING (2)

Hardly a folly but a large domed building, once a full working observatory, housing the advanced equipment necessary for Fuller's much loved hobby, astronomy. Designed by his friend and well known architect, Sir Robert Smirke, the building was completed in 1818. It has since been used for a number of things including a museum. At present it is a private residence, situated south of the Obelisk.

THE SUGAR LOAF, WOODS CORNER (3)

Sited in the middle of a field by the B2096 road, just east of Woods Corner, is a curious thirty-five foot conical structure. A lovely tale surrounds it. Supposedly,

'Mad Jack' wagered that Dallington Church spire could be seen from his home, Rose Hill in Brightling. Discovering he was wrong, he quickly had a building of a similar shape erected on the skyline, thus enabling him to win the wager. The Sugar Loaf has a window and a door and was actually lived in by a farmworker in the late 19th century. A public footpath passes right by the building and it's only a short walk to reach it.

The Sugar Loaf.

THE ROTUNDA TEMPLE, BRIGHTLING PARK (4)

In the middle of the landscaped Brightling Park is the Rotunda Temple. Thought to be designed by Sir Robert Smirke in 1800, it stands at twenty-five foot high, is circular and domed with classical pillars surrounding the inner room. The base is hollow, indicating it could have been used for storage; as for the rest - well, legend takes care of that by suggesting this is where Fuller entertained his lady friends of somewhat dubious character. To see the Temple, one must follow the bridlepath leading off the road, a short distance south of Brightling. The track is almost opposite the Tower (see below) and the walk is about three quarters of a mile.

THE TOWER, BRIGHTLING (5)

By the road just south of Brightling, stands a thirty-five foot stone tower; twelve feet in diameter with windows and a staircase. It was supposedly erected in connection with Fuller's purchase of Bodiam Castle, in 1828. A great deal of restoration was need to the crumbling castle walls and in order to keep an eye on the progress made by his workmen, Fuller had the tower built. Presumably, he must have watched them through a powerful telescope, pinched from his Observatory!

The Tower can be visited and the views across Darwell Reservoir, towards Bodiam, are well worth the climb up the iron staircase.

ROSE HILL, BRIGHTLING (6)

In Brightling, adjacent to the church, one can catch a glimpse of Fuller's superb Georgian mansion, Rose Hill. In 1697, John Fuller, a forbear of Mad Jack, purchased the property. He subsequently had it demolished, rebuilt and then promptly gave the house to his nephew, who called it Rose Hill after his wife, Elizabeth Rose. It eventually passed to their two sons who in turn bequeathed it to John Fuller (Mad Jack), their nephew.

The Pyramid, Mad Jack Fuller's mausoleum.

THE PYRAMID (7)

In the churchyard, competing for importance with the church, is a rather hideous, twenty-five foot Pyramid. It contrasts oddly with the quaint cottages that make up this rural hamlet. This is Fuller's own mausoleum, built twenty-four years before his death in 1834. Why he prepared for his death so early, is still a mystery. However, the outrageous tales attributed to 'Mad Jack' continued to follow him long after he'd died. It was said he had been entombed in his mausoleum sitting in a chair, clutching a top hat and a bottle of claret. In reality, he was buried in the customary fashion beneath the floor.

BRIGHTLING CHURCH (8)

Do visit the church on which Fuller bestowed both time and money. In 1820, he commissioned W.A.A. Nichols to make the organ that is still used today. When it was installed, Fuller presented the male members of the choir with white smocks, buckskin breeches and yellow stockings, whilst the girls had red cloaks: all had to be worn when the organ played. In 1815, he had the church bells re-cast and a new treble added. Three years later, he gave two more bells, making a peal of eight. One bears the inscription - "This peal of bells was completed A.D. 1818 at the expense of John Fuller Esq.," A bust of him presides over the church interior.

THE ESTATE WALL (9)

The great estate wall, some four miles in length, begins at Rose Hill, passes the church, then continues to surround Brightling Park. Started about 1815 when unemployment was high, it provided work for the local people for several years and is supposed to have cost Fuller about £10,000 in labour.

The Southdowns Tour

THE GAMEKEEPER'S TOWER, FIRLE (10)

Sited near the foot of Firle Beacon, this crenellated tower was erected in 1819 for the gamekeeper on the Firle Estate. Internally, it consists of three wedge-shaped bedrooms, a circular kitchen and a circular sitting room. Apparently the reason for building such odd accommodation was so the gamekeeper could signal with ease to the other estate workers. To reach this folly will entail a half mile walk. Follow the sign to Firle, indicated from the A27 road. Once in the village, park the car and take the

Gamekeeper's Tower, Firle.

eastward footpath by the Post Office. This leads past the stately Firle Place (it is open to the public) and through the surrounding parkland. Cross a bridlepath by some cottages, continue up the hill and the gamekeeper's Tower will be directly ahead.

THE LONG MAN, WILMINGTON (11)

The origins of this hill carving are still uncertain. He is approximately 226 feet high and the first records show him holding a scythe and a rake instead of staves. Could he have been carved during Neolithic times or during the 13th century, to indicate the Benedictine Priory in Wilmington? The historians are still puzzled by his existence. Perhaps this delightful piece of folklore provides the answer. Once upon a time there were two giants, one lived on Firle Beacon, the other on Windover Hill. They quarrelled and Firle giant threw a great boulder at Windover giant and killed him. To this day he lies etched in chalk on Windover Hill.

The Long Man is easily visible from the road, but there is a car park in Wilmington (signed from the A27) and it is then only a short walk to this giant figure. Do also visit the pretty little church which has the customary yew tree outside; except that this one is a thousand years old. Nearby is the partially ruined Wilmington Priory, unfortunately not open to the public.

LULLINGTON CHURCH (12)

On a small hill overlooking the Cuckmere Valley is the atmospheric Lullington Church, its white painted belfry peeping above the trees. Dating from the 13th century, it is simply a part of a much larger church, thought to have been destroyed during the time of Cromwell. All that is left is the chancel. Charming in its rural simplicity, the interior measures twenty -three feet by eighteen feet. It seats twenty people and services are held once a month.

THE WHITE HORSE, LITLINGTON (13)

Soon after Litlington village, the road drops to the floor of the valley and away to the west is a great sweep of downland, called 'Hindover' or, more appropriately 'High and Over'. Perched on the side of this escarpment rests the chalk carving of a horse. Done during the 19th century by a James Pagden (and friends) of Alfriston, it was somehow completed overnight, after an evening of heavy drinking. Today it is something of a landmark and kept preserved by the National Trust.

BELLE TOUT, NEAR EASTBOURNE (14)

On the A259, Seaford to Eastbourne road, turn right at East Dean towards the coast. Shortly after Birling Gap, you will see a lighthouse on the cliff top. This is Belle Tout, originally constructed by John Fuller (of Fuller's Follies) in 1834. This inaugural edifice fell into disrepair and had to be demolished. A new lighthouse was erected on the same site. Both proved to be somewhat of a mistake, as they were frequently engulfed by swirling mists and therefore fairly useless. Finally a new lighthouse, which operated

Belle Tout, near Beachy Head.

automatically, was built at the foot of the cliffs. Belle Tout has been converted into an unusual private residence with an Art Deco influenced interior and stunning views of the Sussex coastline.

MARTELLO TOWER, SEAFORD (15)

At the foot of the cliffs, on Seaford's stark and windy seafront is the Martello Tower, one of many built along the south coast to defend the country against Napoleon. The Seaford Martello Tower was completed in 1810. By then the threat of an invasion had passed and the building became redundant. The records of 1873 state the tower was in a 'poor condition' and about to be swept away by rough seas. In 1880, the War Office sold it. By 1910 the dry moat was being used as a roller skating rink and the tower as a tea room. In 1922 an extra storey was added to the top of it for private accommodation.

During the seventies, it was purchased by Lewes District Council, who removed the 'extra storey' and restored the building to the original form. Today it's a museum, filled with information and artefacts on Seaford's interesting and often turbulent history. The Martello Tower is open on Wednesdays, Saturdays and Sundays throughout the season and there is a small admission charge.

THE MARKET CROSS, ALFRISTON (16)

In the centre of ancient Alfriston is the Market Cross, erected during the reign of Henry IV, when the village was granted the right to hold a weekly market. A Market Cross (there is another in Chichester) was a sign to all those who traded nearby, "must do so honestly and fairly". Although not apparent, the Cross has been rather mutilated over the years. About 1830 a round mushroom shaped stone replaced the cross at the top. At the beginning of the century, three old steps were removed, because they obstructed traffic and in 1955 a lorry crashed into it, leaving a pile of rubble behind. The Market Cross has now been rebuilt, but the shaft is of new stone and much shorter.

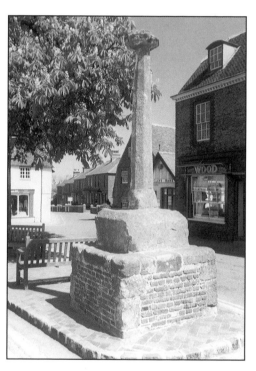

Market Cross, Alfriston.

THE FLINT TOWER, ALFRISTON (17)

A curious flint tower possessing a number of theories as to its original use. Built around 1800, when the Duke of Wellington had some troops stationed in Alfriston, one can probably assume it was something to do with them, but what? Could it have been a lead shot tower, the openings being for lighting and relining the furnace? Maybe, yet it's hardly tall enough for a shot tower. Could it have been a gun store? After all, today's car park was yesterday's parade ground for the troops. A strong possibility (and my favourite), is the tower was used as the local 'lock-up' for naughty soldiers. Although, on the map of 1873, it's marked as a dovecote! Have a look round and make your choice, it's sited in Dene car park.

LITERARY SUSSEX

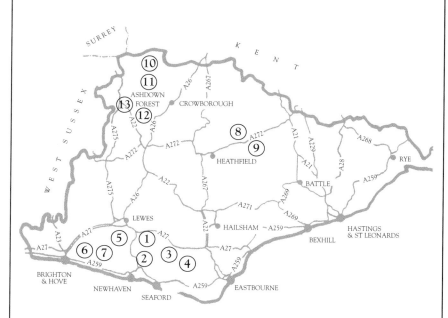

EAST SUSSEX

THE VIRGINIA WOOLF TOUR
1. Firle
2. Asham House
3. Charleston
4. Berwick Church
5. Monks House - Rodmell

THE KIPLING TOUR
6. The Elms - Rottingdean
7. The Grange - Rottingdean
8. Burwash
9. Bateman's - near Burwash

THE A.A. MILNE TOUR
10. Pooh Corner - Hartfield
11. Pooh Sticks Bridge
12. Pooh's Enchanted Place - Gills Lap
13. The Ashdown Forest Centre

LITERARY SUSSEX

Three famous authors, who for the majority of their working lives were resident in East Sussex. The first, Virginia Woolf, was one of the inaugural four (the others being her sister and two brothers) that established the ' Bloomsbury Group'; the name taken from the part of London they lived in. It was to their houses that like-minded artists, writers and intellectuals, such as Maynard Keynes, T.S. Eliot, Lytton Strachey, Roger Fry, to name but a few, came to visit. They discussed each other intimately, they discussed their work at length, they discussed politics and, by standards of the early 20th century, were very 'way out'. Virginia was a complex character and in spite of being plagued by depression, wrote some brilliant literature.

The second author, Rudyard Kipling, came to Sussex in 1897. He was born in Bombay in 1865, then having completed his education in England, returned to India to work for several years. By 1892 he had married and achieved literary success in London. He then spent five years in America before finally settling in Sussex, where most of his well-known works (apart from The Jungle Book) were written. In 1907 he was awarded the Nobel Prize for Literature.

The third author, Alan. A. Milne, created the gloriously whimsical tales and poetry about the childhood of his young son, Christopher Robin and his teddy-bear, Winnie-the-Pooh. A.A.Milne moved to Sussex in 1924 and much of his inspiration came from the beautiful Ashdown Forest that surrounded his home, Cotchford Farm. His early career was spent as Assistant Editor of Punch. He wrote some reasonably successful plays, but fame was finally achieved when his first book, 'When We Were Very Young', sold more than a quarter of a million copies in The United States alone.

The Virginia Woolf Tour

" The days of October melt into each other ....
We begin with mist and end with mist."

FIRLE (1)

Virginia Stephen wrote the above at Firle in 1911. Aged twenty-nine, she was recovering from what was to be one of her many bouts of recurring mental depression. She had taken a lease on the Edwardian Talland House in Firle; this she later admitted to Leonard Woolf was 'a hideous suburban villa', and did not meet the requirements of a rural retreat. Nevertheless, the rest of the village was delightful and 16th century, well positioned in the folds of the Downs she loved. These she explored at length with Leonard.

Firle, indicated from the A27, is a part of the estate owned by the Gage family. They have lived at Firle Place since the 15th century. To this day, it remains a pleasing example of a tied village, with a mere handful of properties being privately owned. This includes Talland House, whose Edwardian architecture is so out of keeping with the other surrounding cottages. In the churchyard, the graves of Vanessa Bell (Virginia's sister) and Duncan Grant can be found.

ASHAM HOUSE (2)

The move from Talland House, where Virginia soon became restless, took place in 1912. She and Leonard had discovered a large house of gracious proportions with tall French windows opening onto the lower slopes of Itford Hill, just west of Firle. Enquiries to the local farmer revealed it was untenanted and he would, at present, be agreeable to sub-letting it. Virginia acquired Asham with a five year lease. In that same year Leonard and Virginia finally married and went to Europe for an extended honeymoon. Whilst abroad, Virginia's sister, Vanessa Bell, moved into the house and set about making it comfortable for them. Although much of her time was spent in their London home, Virginia adored Asham. There were many friends from the 'Bloomsbury Group' who visited or stayed, quite prepared to put up with the inconveniences of country living. Leonard once wrote, "the house had an atmosphere that was romantic, gentle, melancholy - and lovely." An all-embracing combination.

Regrettably, Asham House has now been demolished to make way for the 21st century. But it didn't go without a great deal of resistance from Bloomsbury fans. Blue Circle, who own the site, which is now a rubbish tip, eventually offered a donation of more than £600,000 to locally related projects; only then would Virginia's shadowy ghost allow the bulldozers entry.

CHARLESTON (3)

In 1916, Vanessa leased Charleston Farmhouse, near Firle, some two miles from Virginia at Asham. The two sisters met frequently in Firle for a picnic or visited each other at their homes. Charleston had been empty and neglected for several

Charleston Farmhouse.

years and conditions were primitive; no electricity or plumbing, not even a loo. When Vanessa had managed to make it reasonably habitable, she was joined by her two sons, Quentin and Julian, Duncan Grant (artist and her lover), David (Bunny) Garnett, his friend and occasionally, Clive Bell, her husband. Together they contributed all but the basic structure that is preserved at Charleston today. "If it stood still, they painted it," somebody once remarked. It's true but Charleston has a warmth and a style all of its own, so do make sure to visit this Bloomsbury time warp. Vanessa lived on at Charleston until her death in 1961. Duncan remained there until 1977. He died in 1978.

Charleston is indicated by a brown tourist sign on the A27 between Firle and Berwick. It is open from April until October and there is an admission charge.

BERWICK CHURCH (4)

A beautiful church filled with unusual wall paintings by Vanessa Bell, Quentin Bell and Duncan Grant. Although not strictly on Virginia's tour, for they were not completed until a year after her death in 1942, it's all a part of the 'Bloomsbury syndrome' and it would be a shame to miss it. Information on the paintings can be found in the church guide.

MONK'S HOUSE, RODMELL (5)

In 1919, the farmer required Asham once more and Virginia had to face the prospect of leaving her beloved retreat. On the spur of the moment, she bought the Round House, a converted mill, in Lewes for £300, (see Industrial Sussex). She never lived there; realizing her mistake, when she showed the property to Leonard

Monk's House, Rodmell.

a few weeks later, it was put back on the market. They wanted a cottage in the country, not in a town. But fate looked kindly on them, for on that same day they saw an advertisement for Monk's House in Rodmell, a village that lay on the other side of the River Ouse from Asham. Decision taken and Monk's House was purchased at auction by a local agent on the Woolfs behalf for £700.

Monk's House was much smaller than Asham and like Charleston, basic and primitive. Dating from the 16th century and clad with timber, the rooms were (and still are) rather poky dark and damp. Although Leonard loved the large rambling garden, neither really liked the actual cottage. However, as time went on, improvements were made, their attitude changed and slowly, they grew to love the house. They added a rather strange extension on to the eastern end, consisting of Virginia's bedroom and sitting room, neither being accessible from the house, only from the garden.

At the outbreak of war in 1939, the Woolfs made Monk's House their permanent home. After the severe winter that followed, Virginia suffered influenza and bronchitis. But this was nothing compared to her bouts of mental depression that hovered threateningly below the surface. In March 1941 she left Monk's House for the last time and walked along the Ouse valley until she was almost opposite Asham. With her pockets filled with stones, she waded into the River Ouse and drowned. She was fifty-nine. The coroner's verdict concluded that the lady took her own life whilst of unsound mind. Her last book, 'Between the Acts' was published posthumously. Thereafter, Leonard spent more time in London, visiting Rodmell only occasionally. He died in 1969, aged eighty-nine.

Rodmell is on the A275, Lewes to Newhaven road. There is an admission charge to see Monk's House, which is open on Wednesdays and Saturdays throughout the season.

The Kipling Tour

" Five and twenty ponies, trotting through the dark,
Brandy for the parson, Baccy for the clerk ...."

THE ELMS, ROTTINGDEAN (6)

When Rudyard Kipling returned to England in 1897, he and his family stayed at Prospect House in Rottingdean, near Brighton. This belonged to Kipling's aunt, Georgina Burne-Jones, wife of pre-Raphaelite artist, Edward Burne-Jones. Kipling was so taken with the village that he rented The Elms, an unpretentious house behind a high wall, next to the village green. He wrote several of his famous works here, often sitting in his beautiful gardens. However, he could not secure the privacy he desired and in 1902, retreated to a stately stone house deep in the countryside surrounding Burwash.

The Elms is not open to the public, but the adjoining gardens are, (see Flora and Fauna).

THE GRANGE, ROTTINGDEAN (7)

This handsome Georgian building, now a Museum and Art Gallery, exudes a faded charm; the long shuttered windows facing westwards, look across the village green. The Grange started life as a vicarage and it was not until 1908 that the church sold the property. In 1910, the artist and friend of Kipling, Sir William Nicholson, purchased The Grange and lived there until 1914. A number of owners followed and after wartime service it fell into disrepair, eventually to be bought by the Brighton Corporation. Today, having been fully restored, the Museum and Gallery are managed by the Rottingdean Preservation Society. There are informative

The Grange Museum, Rottingdean.

displays on the local history and famous residents of Rottingdean, in particular Kipling. He commands an exhibition all to himself, with his life-like figure seated at a desk, poised to write. The Grange is open throughout the year, but note - p.m. only on Sundays.

BURWASH (8)

A picturesque, tree-lined village on the A265 Heathfield road, with a good selection of shops and places to eat. At the eastern end of the High Street is the War Memorial, standing in a prominent position by the church. Look at the names carefully; amongst others is that of John Kipling, Rudyard Kipling's son, killed at the Battle of Loos in 1915, aged eighteen years. In the church is a bronze tablet to his memory.

BATEMAN'S, BURWASH (9)

Lying about one mile south of Burwash is Bateman's, an impressive 17th century house, built of local sandstone with mullioned windows and brick chimneys. Not a great deal is known about its early history, but it is generally presumed it was built for an ironmaster. The Kiplings purchased the property in 1902 and carried out considerable restoration work, including installing their own electricity by harnessing the waters of the nearby Dudwell river. In Kipling's autobiography, he

tells with joy of "The very own house. We found," he says "no shadows of ancient regrets, stifled miseries nor any other menace." It answered all his requirements: set amidst delightful scenery, it provided both the peace and privacy so lacking at Rottingdean.

Kipling lived at Bateman's until his death in 1936. He was survived by his wife for three years and it was she who left the entire estate to The National Trust, as a memorial to her husband, our 'Poet of Empire'. Bateman's is open from April until October and the admission includes the house, gardens, oast houses and watermill.

The A. A. Milne Tour

" Wherever I am, there's always Pooh,
There's always Pooh and me ……"

POOH CORNER, HARTFIELD (10)

The attractive village of Hartfield on the B2026 road, has now been immortalized by the author A. A Milne. At the southern end of the High Street is a charming, low ceilinged Queen Anne premises; this is Pooh Corner. When Christopher Robin Milne paid his weekly visit to this little sweet shop with his nanny 'Alice', he probably stocked up on Bullseyes (his favourite sweets), for those memorable trips into Ashdown Forest: the forest that inspired the adventures of Winnie-the-Pooh, Piglet, Eeyore, Tigger and Christopher Robin himself.

Pooh Corner is open every day and is full of very tempting 'Pooh-phanalia' souvenirs on sale. The Pooh books transport one back to the days of childhood and what's more, you can still buy Bullseyes from the old glass jars.

POOH STICKS BRIDGE (11)

It's only five minutes by car from Hartfield to the car park that serves Pooh Sticks Bridge, but it's easy to go wrong - well, I found it easy. From Pooh Corner look right to where the road forks. Once in the car, take the left hand fork signed to Maresfield. At Chuck Hatch, which is after about two miles, turn right and the car park is almost immediately on the right. It is then about a three-quarters of a mile walk to Pooh Sticks Bridge. The woodland track is well signed but can be muddy. Collect some twigs on the way, so you can play Christopher Robin's favourite game of 'Pooh Sticks' when you reach the bridge. It's fun.

POOH'S ENCHANTED PLACE, GILLS LAP (12)

Gills Lap car park is located at the junction of the Hartfield and Coleman's Hatch roads on the B2026. Having parked, walk directly north along the wide track. The rising ground to the left is Pooh's 'Enchanted Place' and it's also here you'll find the 'Heffalump Trap', the 'Sandpit' and a view of Christopher Robin's '100 Aker Wood'. After about half a mile, in a secluded spot with a magnificent panorama, is the memorial stone to A. A. Milne, the author and E. H. Shepard, the illustrator of Winnie-the-Pooh books. This is one of the loveliest areas of Ashdown Forest, ideal for walking or simply having a picnic.

Memorial stone and plaque, Gills Lap.

THE ASHDOWN FOREST CENTRE (13)

The above Centre is near Wych Cross on the Coleman's Hatch road. It has an excellent section on Christopher Robin, his friends and their adventures in Ashdown Forest. (See Flora and Fauna for additional information).

FOUR RIVERS AND THEIR SECRETS

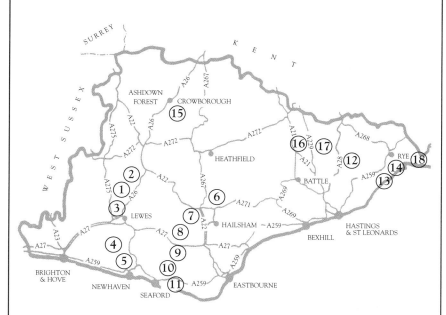

EAST SUSSEX

THE OUSE TOUR
1. Barcombe Mills
2. The Anchor Inn
3. Hamsey
4. Southease
5. Newhaven Harbour

THE CUCKMERE TOUR
6. Hellingly
7. Michelham Priory
8. Arlington Reservoir
9. The Cuckmere Valley
10. Alfriston
11. Cuckmere Haven

THE BREDE TOUR
12. Brede
13. Royal Military Canal
14. Camber Castle

THE ROTHER TOUR
15. Rotherfield
16. Salehurst
17. Bodiam Castle
18. Rye Harbour

FOUR RIVERS AND THEIR SECRETS

A theme that follows the meanders of four Sussex rivers and visits interesting and unusual, yet lesser known, places sited on their banks. The Ouse and the Rother are certainly the longest rivers. The Ouse, the most westerly, rises in St. Leonard's Forest, near Horsham in West Sussex and arrives in East Sussex near Fletching. It then makes its way through the levels, before passing the county town of Lewes and reaching the sea at the port of Newhaven. The Rother, having risen in the hilly landscape near Rotherfield, sweeps into a sort of semicircle and crossing marshland forms a part of the Sussex/Kent border before entering the sea near Rye.

The Cuckmere and the Brede are smaller Sussex rivers. The Cuckmere has two sources, one at Heathfield and one at Possingworth; both are about five hundred feet above sea level, so the river descends considerably before it reaches the sea and striking scenery at Cuckmere Haven. The Brede, which is even smaller than the Cuckmere, passes through the idyllic countryside north of Hastings and together with the River Tillingham, flows into the Rother at Rye.

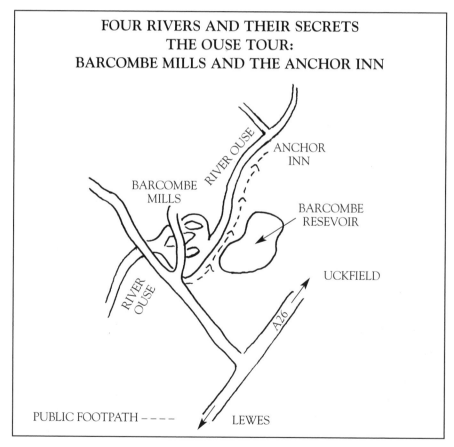

FOUR RIVERS AND THEIR SECRETS
THE OUSE TOUR:
BARCOMBE MILLS AND THE ANCHOR INN

44

The Ouse Tour

BARCOMBE MILLS (1)

Let's join the river at Barcombe Mills, a few miles after it reaches East Sussex. This fascinating, historically complex and delightful spot is near the A26, on the Lewes to Uckfield road. It consists of some cottages, a farm, several barns and Barcombe House, all sited by the River Ouse and its maze of surrounding waterways. The weir, the canals, the sluice gates and the trout pool are all man made. It is now a favourite haunt for anglers. Many years ago it was a working river and horse drawn barges were pulled towards the mill that was astride the main stream. The largest bridge overlooks the weir. This leaves the main river above the mill and rejoins it just below. It was cut so that the water could by-pass the mill when power was not needed and is called a 'head and tail stream'. On the downstream side is the site of the old mill that burned down in 1939. The miller, who owned the road as well, charged tolls; a copy is still there and reads:-

Carriage and Horse	1s 0d
Four Wheels and one Horse	9d
Two Wheels and one Horse	6d
Wagon and Horses	1s 6d
Steam Engines	2s 0d
Motor Cycle & Side Car	3d

Beneath Pike's Bridge runs a short canal, joining the loop of the main river. Exceptionally high tides reached here and barges had to be raised about 20 feet. Two locks were installed; these are now fish ladders and you can actually see the trout leap one step at a time. A walk around the waterways or simply sitting by the river, watching the fish and listening to the weir, is a very pleasant way of passing the time.

THE ANCHOR INN (2)

At Barcombe Mills, follow the river footpath upstream past Barcombe Reservoir and through the meadows for one mile and you'll find The Anchor Inn. It can't be missed. This unusual public house, reputed to be the smallest in England, is right on the river. Built in 1790, it originally catered for bargees, whose horse drawn barges travelled from Newhaven to Slaugham. The Anchor has exclusive boating rights over a stretch of the Ouse, extending to 'fish ladder falls'. The boats, moored outside, can be hired from the inn and a round trip takes a leisurely two hours.

HAMSEY (3)

Hamsey is indicated on the A275 road at Offham, north of Lewes. Having turned into the lane, bear right after the railway line. There is not really much of Hamsey now and what is left clutches on to a low lying hill, almost entirely surrounded by the River Ouse. One has the oddest feeling of being marooned. It is accessible only by crossing a canal cut and passing through Hamsey Place farmyard. A farm that appears bleak, unmodernised and unaffected by time. The 12th century church has the same atmosphere of desolation. Presumably this windswept hillock was once the site of the Norman village of Hamsey; the cause of its abandonment still unknown. Perhaps the hollow-eyed gargoyles that stare eerily across the Sussex levels from the church tower, know the reason? The church is kept locked, but can be visited by collecting the key from the farm.

From Hamsey it is only a short distance to Lewes, where the river passes through a gap in the downland, east of the town and then flows into the broad reaches of the Ouse valley, before reaching Newhaven.

SOUTHEASE (4)

A secluded and peaceful hamlet, about three miles north of Newhaven and centred mainly around the sloping village green. The tiny Norman church has an unusual rounded tower, one of three in Sussex, the others being at Piddinghoe and Lewes. There is a transitional chancel arch and the remains of once vivid 13th century wall paintings. Southease appears to have a medieval atmosphere all of its own; a carthorse and wagon, filled with hay, would not look amiss. A few minutes walk from the village are the wide sweeps of the river Ouse, the old swing bridge, fishponds and canals. The upstream towpath will take you to Lewes and it makes a very pretty walk through the 'brooks' and meadow land abutting the river. The stretch of downland immediately opposite the swing bridge is Itford Hill. Some years ago a bronze age settlement was discovered there and it is now rated as a key archaeological site. Records suggest that in Domesday, when Southease was owned by an Abbey near Winchester, 38,500 herring used to be paid in annual rent. Does this mean it was once a fishing village?

Southease Church, with its unusual round tower.

NEWHAVEN HARBOUR (5)

Oh, the excitement of a harbour; the hustle, bustle and noise of boats, little boats, sailing boats, passenger ships and freight ships. There is always something to watch, especially at Newhaven, for it's a busy port with the large ferries making several daily trips to Dieppe and back. Today, this is where the mouth of the Ouse enters the sea; but it has not always been so. At one time, it entered the sea at Seaford, three miles away. Legend suggests a violent storm in 1579, altered the course of the river overnight, causing it to break through at Newhaven, and suddenly, Seaford was no longer a port. Research however, indicates a little differently. During the fifteenth century a larger type of vessel was being built and these were unable to cross the shingle bar at Seaford Harbour. This coupled with widespread flooding in the Ouse valley, meant action by man and not fate, was necessary. An ambitious project went ahead for cutting a 'new haven' into the sea, long before the river reached Seaford, thus allowing it to flow freely, reduce the flooding and also provide a larger deeper port.

Apart from watching the comings and goings of seafaring traffic at Newhaven Harbour, there are clifftop footpaths, shingle beaches and a sandy cove for the kids to swim from, if it's warm enough. Alternatively there is a fort, built into the chalk hillside, or the local maritime museum to visit; or perhaps a bracing walk along the impressive breakwater that is almost one third of a mile long. Whatever, don't forget to buy some fresh fish, straight from the sea, for sale from the little wooden huts sited on the quayside.

Newhaven Harbour.

The Cuckmere Tour

HELLINGLY (6)

This attractive village, two miles north of Hailsham, is the meeting place for the two head streams of the Cuckmere, the sources being at Possingworth and Heathfield. Hellingly is dominated by a large Norman church set in a delightful churchyard surrounded by trees and quaint cottages. A water mill nestles by the river a short way down Mill Lane and claims to be the oldest water mill in England. It was last used for milling in 1919 and in the 1930's was advertised as 'The Old Watermill Tearooms'. The complex is now privately owned. The 'Cuckoo Trail', a landscaped walk and cycle way along a disused railway track, passes immediately behind the mill and access is from the lane.

MICHELHAM PRIORY (7)

A loop, plus a little help from man, has diverted the river to form a 6 1/2 acre moat, one of the largest in England, around this 13th century Augustinian Priory. The only approach to Michelham, having passed a water mill, is via a 14th century gatehouse. Beyond lies landscaped gardens, medieval barns and the Priory itself. The entirety belongs to the Sussex Archaeological Society and it is open from Easter to the end of October. An admission is charged and frequently concerts, exhibitions and lectures are held here throughout the season.

Michelham Priory

ARLINGTON RESERVOIR (8)

Arlington Reservoir covers about 120 acres and was designed by the East Sussex County Council as a Nature Reserve. It was completed by the Eastbourne Water Company in 1971 and supplies all the local areas. It is also a private trout fly fishery. The reservoir was formed by blocking a meander in the river with a dam.

Afterwards, the surrounds were planted with more than 30,000 trees, including oak, birch, wild cherry, hazel, willow, mountain ash and hawthorn. The footpaths around the reservoir are exceptionally pretty and the Downs provide a superb backdrop. There is parking and information at the reservoir, sited about a mile and a half from the A27, just north of Berwick Station.

THE CUCKMERE VALLEY (9)

For the final part of its journey, the Cuckmere heads for a break in the backbone of downland. Now, it is only about four miles to the sea, Do explore those four miles, either on foot or by car; for the roads (or paths) travel through some of the loveliest hamlets and countryside you could wish to see.

ALFRISTON (10)

This historic village, a mile or so south of the A27, is hardly a secret; it is one of the most visited and one of the most beautiful villages in East Sussex. Alfriston lies on a curve in the river near the head of the Cuckmere valley, watched over by the imposing St. Andrews Church, built on the Tye at the waters edge. Nearby, at White Bridge, ducks, swans and geese gather, hoping for food. Less than a hundred years ago, a wharf lay there too; for the river was navigable by barges up to this point. Small pleasure craft continued to use the river until the 60's; now it's the occasional canoe. The pretty footpaths either side of the river banks ultimately lead to the sea at Cuckmere Haven. Alfriston has acquired the title of being like an 'open air museum'. Some of the buildings, which date from the 14th century, now accommodate shops, tearooms and pubs. There is plenty for the visitor to do and see.

CUCKMERE HAVEN (11)

The mouth of the river culminates in reeded meanders, salt marshes and rolling downland; this forms one of the most scenic stretches of coastal landscape in England. To the east are the chalk cliffs, sculpted by erosion to form seven hills, named 'The Seven Sisters'. To the west, the old coastguard cottages perch precariously on the cliff edge; beyond is Hope Gap, a cove once used by smugglers and the sheer cliffs of Seaford Head. Years ago, the natural path of the river was to follow the meanders; this caused shingle, driven from west to east by the prevailing wind, to block the mouth. Widespread flooding occurred and eventually man had to intervene by 'canalizing' or straightening the river south of Exceat Bridge. Cuckmere Haven is situated near Seaford on the A259 road to Eastbourne. On the eastern side of the valley are two car parks and a collection of flint barns. These house an excellent Visitor Centre which can supply all the necessary information about the area. In the adjacent farmhouse is a restaurant and tea room.

The Brede Tour

BREDE (12)

An attractive village, on the A28, with extensive views across the levels, where the river of the same name rises. It looks towards Winchelsea and Rye; here the Brede joins the Rother before reaching the sea. There is a short but very pretty towpath walk downstream from Brede Bridge. St. George's Church, dating from the 12th century, is one of the loveliest rural churches in Sussex. Inside is a tall and unusual wooden statue of The Madonna, carved by the well known sculptor and writer Clare Sheridan. The wood she used come from the parkland of her home, Brede Place and it was sculpted in memory of her son Richard, who died at the age of twenty-one. The bridlepath that passes in front of the church leads along the Brede Valley for about a mile and makes a very pleasant stroll.

ROYAL MILITARY CANAL (13)

Situated at the foot of Winchelsea Hill, adjacent to the A259 to Rye, is the Royal Military Canal. The canal was built between 1804 and 1809 as a defence system across the marshes, which otherwise provided rather too easy access for raids by the French. It begins at the cliffs of Fairlight, near Hastings and stretches across Romney Marshes to Seabrook, in Kent. The Royal Military Canal Path is part of a planned walkway that will eventually run alongside the complete canal. At the moment, two sections are open, from Pett to Iden Lock, which is nine miles and a further five miles, between Stutfall Castle and Seabrook. The canal path is waymarked and signed with a distinctive logo. The yellow arrows indicate footpaths and the blue, bridleways.

Royal Military Canal.

CAMBER CASTLE (14)

Don't miss seeing one of the best kept secrets in East Sussex. The 16th century Camber Castle lies hidden in isolated splendour, close to the River Brede, between Rye and Winchelsea. It's situated on flat marshy land and was built by Henry VIII to defend Rye from possible invasion. It has five circular bastions, a central tower and a network of tunnels. It was completed in 1543. Unfortunately, its use a defence lasted less than a hundred years, due to the receding coastline and in 1640 the castle was abandoned. It fell into ruin and was finally closed off in 1967. Considerable repairs have since been carried out and arrangements to visit Camber Castle can be made through Rye heritage Centre. Alternatively, if you would like a short walk just to see it externally, take the road to Winchelsea Beach. On a particularly sharp right hand bend is a bridlepath on the left. Walk down the path, passing Castle Farm, then take the footpath on the left and continue towards Camber Castle, which can be clearly seen from here. It is not fenced off, so it's possible to explore around the perimeter and peer through grids and gateways to get a reasonably good view of the inside. An excellent spot for a picnic too.

The Rother Tour

ROTHERFIELD (15)

Rotherfield lies on the B2101 road, four miles east of Crowborough. It sits on high ground and overlooks the valley where the River Rother rises. The large early English church has a tall perpendicular spire; a noted landmark for many miles around. In the Neville chapel is a fine example of 19th century pre-Raphaelite glass, placed in the 15th century east window. It was designed by Edward Burne-Jones and made by William Morris and Co. Outside, in the churchyard is the most amazing yew tree; supposed to be 1500 years old, it is almost completely hollow and has to be supported by huge stakes. It must be one of nature's miracles to be so resplendent; certainly an item of interest not to be missed. The village is very pleasant with quaint old properties, a pub and some interesting shops. Its only drawback is the rather too frequent traffic that seems to pass through.

SALEHURST (16)

Set deep in the country lanes, east of the A21 near Robertsbridge, is the tiny hamlet of Salehurst. Built on the upper slopes of the Rother, it has a fine 13th century church, erected by the monks of Robertsbridge. St. Mary's possesses an unusual font, over 700 years old and having a ring of salamanders around the base. The local inn, called The Salehurst Halt, presumably because of the defunct railway line nearby, is one of the best pubs in Sussex; do try and put it on the agenda as a lunch stop. For a short and interesting walk, take the footpath to the right of the church, follow it downhill, cross the bridge over the river and turn left onto a bridlepath. Ahead will be the handsome Abbey Farm, built on the site and incorporating some walls of the Cistercian Robertsbridge Abbey, founded in 1176. Further remains lie behind the farm and these can easily be seen from the public bridlepath.

BODIAM CASTLE (17)

A fairytale 14th century castle rising from a broad moat, carpeted with water lilies and fed by the Rother. The castle, completed in 1388, was built by Sir Edward Dalyngrigge to protect his manor from raids by the French, the river being a navigable estuary at that time. The feared attacks never occurred and Bodiam simply became the rather grand residence for Sir Edward and his family. During the Civil War in the 17th century, much of the interior was despoiled, leaving the ruins neglected and open to all weathers, for three hundred years. In 1916 it was purchased and restored by Lord Curzon and it was he who bequeathed it to the National Trust in 1925. Today it remains in their capable hands, thus ensuring this valuable part of our heritage is well preserved. Bodiam Castle, situated just east of the B2244 road, is open to the public throughout the year. There is an admission charge and in the castle grounds is a tearoom, shop and museum.

RYE HARBOUR (18)

The flat, desolate and beautifully different landscape of Rye Harbour, is situated two miles south east of Rye. The semblance of a village with a few cottages, a local shop, a pub and some low, tarred buildings, is all that's there; apart from fishing smacks or sailing boats pulled up on the mud flats, often at curious angles. The actual mouth of the river is still about a mile away and one must follow the footpath through Rye Harbour Nature Reserve and then along the beach, to get to it. During medieval times the Rother entered the sea just below Rye itself, thus enabling the town to be a wealthy and substantial port. Silting up caused the sea to recede and now only small craft can navigate the river up to Rye.

Rye Harbour Nature Reserve was established in 1970 and is designed to conserve the plants, animals, birds and water life that exist in this lowland area. In the car park at Rye Harbour is an Information Centre with maps, photographs and details about the entire Reserve. When walking here, do look out for the unusual Yellow Horned Sea Poppy; it blooms in profusion from June to October.

Rye Harbour

FLORA AND FAUNA

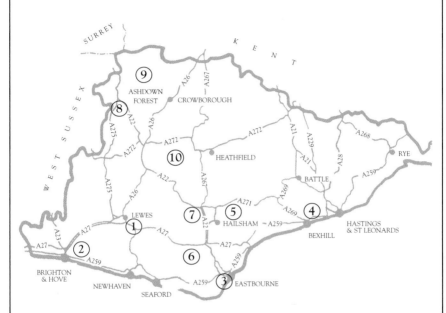

EAST SUSSEX

THE GARDEN TOUR
1. The Grange Gardens - Lewes
2. Kipling Gardens - Rottingdean
3. Holywell Retreat and The Italian
   Gardens - Eastbourne
4. Manor Gardens - Bexhill
5. The Elizabethan Gardens at
   Herstmonceux Castle

THE WILDFLOWER TOUR
6. The Downland Walk - Jevington
7. The Bluebell Walk - Arlington

THE WOODED TOUR
8. The Ashdown Forest Centre
9. Ashdown Forest
10. Wilderness Wood - Hadlow Down

FLORA AND FAUNA

The undiscovered secrets of Flora and Fauna in East Sussex are harboured not only in the rolling downland, but in towns, woods and lowlands. The Garden Tour travels to three town gardens, all located in historical settings, beautifully landscaped and free; yet they remain relatively empty. Another garden is set in the little seaside village of Rottingdean, adjacent to Kipling's old home; that is free, too. The extensive Elizabethan gardens of Herstmonceux Castle complete the route and offer an interesting insight to gardening in the Tudor era. There is an admission charge for this one.

The glorious Wildflower Tour takes the form of a circular six mile walk across the Downs between Eastbourne and Alfriston. This lasts a full day and travels across some of the most scenic terrain in Sussex. The Bluebell Walk, harboured in the upper reaches of the Cuckmere Valley, is an 'extra' only as the season is so short; it is however, particularly pretty so do try not to miss it. A favourite for children too.

The Wooded Tour is set in the High Weald. Here the trails in and around Ashdown Forest can last just as long as you want them to; there is so much to see and it is definitely one of the finest areas in the South for walkers, cyclists and naturalists. Do visit the first class Forest Centre to collect any necessary information before setting off on a trail. A trip to Wilderness Wood at Hadlow Down shows the traditional methods of growing and using timber.

On a final note, if you only have a couple of hours to spare, why not visit Sheffield Park Gardens owned by the National Trust and situated mid way between Lewes and East Grinstead, east of the A275. Here there is a glorious mixture of woodland, formal gardens and wildflowers. Designed around five lakes by Capability Brown, Sheffield Park Gardens have become famous for the spring displays of rhododendrons and azaleas. An admission is charged.

The Garden Tour

THE GRANGE GARDENS, LEWES (1)

Southover Grange, only minutes from the railway station, nestles peacefully in the shadows of the ancient hill town of Lewes. This provides an intriguing backdrop of rising terracotta rooftops, curiously twisted chimney pots and slender church spires. The mellow Elizabethan house, built in 1572 of Caen stone, faces southwards across stone flagged terraces, cream magnolias and copper beeches, to the vibrant hues of the herbaceous borders beyond. It was occupied by the Newton family, uninterruptedly until 1860. The diarist, John Evelyn, a distant relative, lived there as a boy, from 1630 to 1637, whilst he attended the old Grammar School. In 1871, William Laird Macgregor purchased the property and carried out extensive alterations. He then took an instant dislike to the place and never set foot in it again. Thereafter, it had a number of owners. In 1974, The Grange came into the possession of Lewes District Council and now, amongst other things, houses some craft workshops and the local Registry Offices. The walled and beautifully kept gardens are open every day until dusk and display an enormous variety of flowers, shrubs and trees in an idyllic setting. On the main lawn is a splendid example of a North American Tulip Tree, thought to be the oldest in this country.

Grange Gardens, Lewes.

KIPLING GARDENS, ROTTINGDEAN (2)

A particularly attractive village, built in a valley or 'dene' (hence the name Rottingdean), leading from the sea on to downland. The properties, many of them Georgian, are clustered around the village green, making it a delightful place to visit, except for the traffic. In season, the narrow streets become particularly congested and parking can be difficult. It was a very different scene when Rudyard Kipling purchased the 18th century house opposite the Green and duck pond in 1897. He lived in 'The Elms' for five years and some of his most famous works were written relaxing in his beautiful gardens. Unfortunately, thereafter, they became derelict and overgrown: plans were drawn up for houses to be built on those very grounds Kipling had loved. At this point, Rottingdean Preservation Society stepped in and stopped the proposed development by purchasing the land and transforming the wilderness back to its former glory. In 1986 the Kipling Gardens were officially opened. This attractive, landscaped two acres, in the heart of Rottingdean, is open every day throughout the year. In all, there are five separate walled areas, including a rose garden, a herb garden and a wild garden; each are adjoined by flint walls, arches and brick paths.

HOLYWELL RETREAT AND THE ITALIAN GARDENS, EASTBOURNE (3)

Tucked against the south-east cliffs leading to Beachy Head are steep, landscaped cliff gardens with narrow paths tumbling down to the hidden, lesser known, but by far the most beautiful part of Eastbourne's seafront. Here the beaches remain quiet and peaceful for most of the year; perhaps that is why it's called 'Retreat'. It was a favourite haunt of King George V and Queen Mary during their stay in 1935 and a plaque marks their chalet. The Italian Gardens, at the end of Holywell Retreat, were built in an old chalk pit during the 1930's. The shady, colonnaded summerhouse looks directly out to sea; a fitting setting for the open air plays that are occasionally performed here. Nearby, the little beach cafe with terraces and colourful umbrellas, makes an excellent refreshment stop. On the cliff tops above, are the Helen Gardens with flowering shrubs, a bowling green, tennis courts and a putting green. Whilst exploring here, don't miss a walk down the unmade up track between Helen Gardens and St. Bede's School. This culminates at steep steps leading to secluded beaches, where the views are breathtaking and shouldn't be missed.

Holywell Retreat, Eastbourne.

MANOR GARDENS, BEXHILL (4)

The history of the old town of Bexhill can be traced back, way beyond the 9th century, when it was a tiny fishing village , perched on a hill and the parish church of St. Peter had just been founded. The Manor of Bexhill, built during the 12th century, belonged to the Sackville family and Manor Gardens lies within the ruins of their early medieval home. The stone arches and walls, even a fireplace still exist, entwined with clematis, passion flower and jasmine. What used to be rooms are now individual gardens linked by the remains of doorways, with flowering shrubs in all the corners. Formal displays of annuals have been planted centrally. These charming and tranquil gardens have been thoughtfully laid out and are lovely and unusual to visit. There is even a scented garden for the blind with explanatory notes in Braille. During the summer months the Sackvilles old flint coach house often provides a backdrop for open air theatre. Their pavilion, which overlooks the rose garden, is used for functions and the former stable block now houses the Bexhill Museum of Costume and Social History; open from April until October.

THE ELIZABETHAN GARDENS AT HERSTMONCEUX CASTLE (5)

Herstmonceux Castle was constructed in the 15th century by Sir Roger Fiennes and appears to combine his love of the French brick chateau, an English castle and a stylish country mansion. It remained in his family until 1708, when it was sold to a George Naylor. Sadly, by the end of the eighteenth century it had fallen into ruins. After a succession of owners, several of them opening the crumbling battlements to visitors and charging sixpence, Sir Paul Latham M.P. purchased the castle and completely restored it. In 1946 the entire estate was bought by the Admiralty to be the new home of The Royal Observatory, Greenwich. Just recently it was sold to Queen's University, Ontario, Canada. The Castle is not open to the public but the surrounding parkland and gardens are; there is an entrance charge. The walled Elizabethan gardens have been beautifully recreated and the herbaceous borders are filled with herbs and traditional English perennials, giving a riot of colour throughout the summer. The gentle sloping lawns and idyllic views make it a pleasant spot for a picnic; or alternatively, there is a good teashop within the castle grounds.

Teazels, Elizabethan Gardens, Herstmonceux.

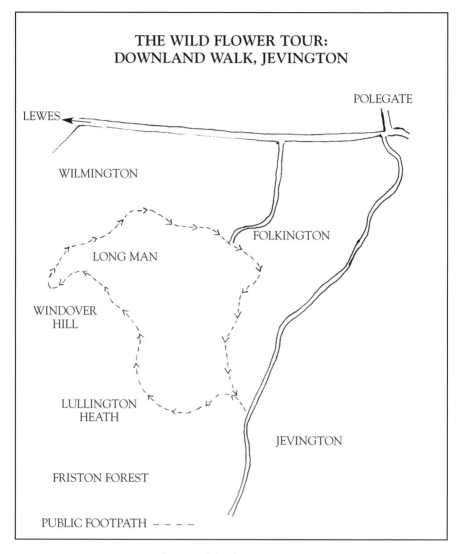

THE WILD FLOWER TOUR: DOWNLAND WALK, JEVINGTON

POLEGATE

LEWES

WILMINGTON

FOLKINGTON

LONG MAN

WINDOVER HILL

LULLINGTON HEATH

JEVINGTON

FRISTON FOREST

PUBLIC FOOTPATH – – – –

The Wild Flower Tour

THE DOWNLAND WALK, JEVINGTON (6)

A circular 6 1/2 mile walk starting by the church in the rural village of Jevington, indicated from the A22 at Polegate, near Eastbourne. Apart from this being one of the most scenic walks in East Sussex, it is also one of the finest for seeing the greatest variety of downland flowers. The public footpaths and bridleways are marked on the Ordnance Survey Pathfinder map, No. 1324 and it is advisable to use one for reference, although the trail is signed. Initially, the footpath travels through the trees above Jevington, before reaching the wide expanses of Lullington Heath Nature Reserve. This reserve was established in 1954 and is one of the largest chalk heathlands remaining in Britain. The areas of yellow gorse and scrub are home to foxes, badgers and rabbits; here they can breed in relative shelter. In summer, butterflies such as marbled white, chalk hill blue, brimstone, and fritillary hover on the flowers. Six different types of orchid have been recorded, including the early purple, spotted and bee orchid. The walk moves on from Lullington Heath to Windover Hill, some 700 feet above sea level. The views are extensive; Friston Forest and the sea at Cuckmere Haven lie to the south-east; Firle Beacon and Mount Caburn to the west and finally the High Weald and Ashdown Forest to the north. In the spring the lower slopes of Windover have a profusion of cowslips growing and in June and July the cornfields below are ablaze with poppies. The footpath now descends to pass below the Long Man (see Folly Spotting for information), continues northwards and finally bears right along a bridleway leading into woodland. This stretch of the walk follows a part of the old Turnpike Road, the route used by stage-coaches (1750 to 1820) from Lewes to Eastbourne. At the pretty village of Folkington, the lane winds to the right again, around the foot of Folkington Hill and then back to Jevington. Here the hedgerows are a hotchpotch of hawthorn, elder, hazel, dog rose and blackberry, whilst the banks are filled with campion, fool's parsley, foxgloves and teasel. This varied landscape also offers something for the birdwatchers too. The kestrel and the skylark frequent the open downland and occasionally, peregrine falcons can be seen circling high in the sky. The woods and meadows provide a natural habitat for woodpeckers, nightingales, buntings, jays and meadow pipits.

DOWNLAND FLOWERS

Orchids: The most common on the chalk downs are the spotted and the pyramidal (military) orchid. The spotted has pale lilac flowers and dark splodges on the leaves.
The pyramidal is deep pink and can grow in abundance. Both flower from June till August.

Wild Thyme: Deep purple, similar to the cultivated type, but much shorter. Flowers throughout the summer.

Milkwort: A small ground hugging flower of a bluish purple hue, found in June and July.

Horse-shoe Vetch: One of the commonest downland plants, its vivid yellow flowers on spreading stems, sometimes up to twelve inches long, can be seen from May until August.

Dropwort: A relative of meadowsweet, favouring a chalky terrain instead of damp fields. Its pinkish white flowers are highly scented and can be found in June and July.

Rampion: Grows in quantity on the Downs during July and August,

	This deep blue flower on slender stems about twelve inches high, is one of the prettiest.
Scabious:	Several lilac coloured flowers born on one stem, varying from one to three feet high, from June to September.
Cowslips:	Delightful yellow scented flowers on stoutish stems about six inches high. The flowering period is during April and May.
Viper's Bugloss:	Found on wasteland and chalky soil, this plant appears to thrive on nothing. The flowers, first reddish, then bright blue, are on rather prickly stems that can grow to about two feet high. It flowers from May to August.
Bird's Foot Trefoil:	These yellow flowers are very similar to that of the Horseshoe Vetch, except they are tinged with red. The seed pods, usually about an inch in length, are in clusters of three or four, resembling a bird's claw; hence the name. It flowers from June to October.
Silverweed:	Found in the moister corners of the Downs, this low growing, silvery leafed plant has single yellow flowers of five petals. Flowering is in the early summer.
Knapweed:	Similar in appearance to a thistle without all the prickly bits. The purple flowers, on slender stems, grow to a height of two or three feet and can be seen from July to September.

THE BLUEBELL WALK, ARLINGTON (7)

A fairytale woodland walk at Bates Green Farm, Arlington; open for just four weeks each year, during the bluebell season of April and May. The six marked trails wander through tended woods, coppices and glades, where the rich carpet of blue, in April mixed with white veined anemones, makes a spectacular scene beneath the trees. The barns at the entrance to the walk have a small selection of farm animals that will keep the children entertained and refreshments are available, too. An entrance fee is charged and the woodland is well signed from the A27 and the A22 during the time it is open. (See back cover).

The Wooded Tour

THE ASHDOWN FOREST CENTRE (8)

This excellent Information Centre has to be the first stop when visiting Ashdown Forest. It is extremely well appointed and has everything you could possibly need to know before exploring the area. There are maps and leaflets on all the forest walks; pamphlets on both the history and natural history; a map and guide to the forest, showing the roads, footpaths, bridleways and parking places; educational questionnaires can be purchased for children too. The interior of the Centre is interestingly laid out with displays on the forest wildlife and plants, plus a small exhibition entitled, 'The Forest at Night'. The only drawback is that the place is rather difficult to find, so here are the directions. Take the A22 from Forest Row and after two miles, turn left at Wych Cross. Follow the road for about a mile and the Centre, which is quite a large barn like structure, is amongst trees on the left, by a car park. It is open all day at weekends throughout the year and weekday afternoons from April to September as well.

ASHDOWN FOREST (9)

A magnificent stretch of forest and heathland with far reaching views, sitting on a high plateau in a sort of triangle, formed by East Grinstead, Groombridge and Uckfield. The highest point

Ashdown Forest Centre.

is over 700 feet above sea level. During the 13th century it was used as a Royal Hunting Ground by John of Gaunt, Duke of Lancaster. At that time the forest was enclosed by a 'pale'. This consisted of a bank, surmounted by a wooden fence and an internal ditch, thus making it easy for deer to jump in and impossible for them to get out. Ashdown Forest continued thereafter, to be used extensively, especially by Henry VIII, for hunting. Sadly by 1657 not a single deer remained. By the end of the 17th century, a great deal of deforestation had also taken place, due to the Great Sussex Ironworks needing wood to turn into charcoal to feed the furnaces. The next two hundred and fifty years saw the forest being exploited by a number of people with conflicting interests. Happily today, the freehold ownership is held by the Ashdown Forest Trust; rangers look after the entirety; new trees have replaced those felled and the deer have returned. The heathland provides a picturesque scene with yellow gorse in the spring and purple heather in the autumn. The trees that can be found in the forest are listed below; don't forget to look for the grey squirrels that inhabit them. Some of the animals and birds are nocturnal, such as foxes, badgers, bats and owls, so a visit at dusk can be unusual and rewarding. The walks are many and varied throughout this area of outstanding natural beauty and the Forest Centre has details for ten, all about 2 1/2 miles. On a clear day, drive to Four Counties Car Park, near Gills Lap; as the name suggests the views span four different counties.

FOREST TREES

Birch: A graceful tree, with a fine whitish silver bark, drooping boughs and slender catkins in the spring.

Beech: The common beech, with a greyish trunk, has been planted on the forest fringes. The nuts provide food for squirrels.

Yew: The thick dark green foliage of a yew is usually associated with a graveyard.
Most of the yew trees in the forest are self sown, probably with the help of birds.

Sweet Chestnut: This tree can grow up to 70 feet high and has deep spiral grooves in the trunk. A good crop of edible nuts, shielded in spiny coats, are found during the autumn.

Rowan: A slender tree with clusters of white flowers in the spring and vivid orange
berries in the autumn.

Oak: The most English of all trees can be found throughout the forest. There are several varieties and the acorns and the leaves differ a little with each specie.

Scots Pine: Our native conifer, too large for the average garden, but it has become a much photographed symbol of Ashdown Forest.

Hazel: This tree has a quick re-growth and is therefore useful for fencing and basketry.

WILDERNESS WOOD, HADLOW DOWN (10)

On the A272, west of Heathfield, lies 60 acres of working woodland, filled with coppices of sweet chestnuts, birches and plantations of pine and beech. The marked footpaths, plus an explanatory map, travel through a terrain that offers a marvellous insight into woodland life. An encounter with a massive beech tree, thought to be about 180 years old, appears unreal, almost as though it were transplanted from a scene in Disneyland. During wet weather, mosses, ferns and liverworts multiply by the streams and bogs, (wellies essential!). Bluebells and foxgloves abound in the spring and summer, fungi and autumnal colours dress the scene in September and October. Pine cones lie strewn across the loamy soil in winter, when between the naked branches one can catch a rewarding glimpse of the extensive views from the High Weald to the South Downs. The woodyard and barn exhibit traditional methods for the use of timber and a number of wood products, grown and made on site, are on sale. In 1993, Wilderness Wood won the Duke of Cornwall's Award for forestry and conservation.

The entire area is open all the year and there is a small entrance charge.

ANTIQUES, BRIC-A-BRAC AND JUNK

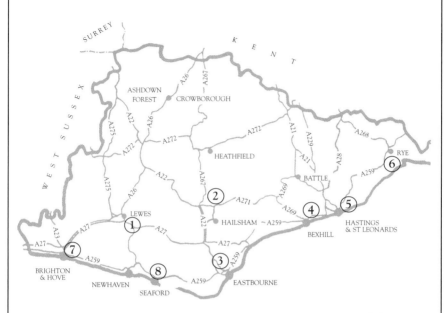

EAST SUSSEX

THE MARKET TOUR
1. Lewes
2. Hailsham
3. Eastbourne

THE COLLECTOR'S TOUR
4. Bexhill
5. Hastings Old Town
6. Rye

THE DEALER'S TOUR
7. Brighton
8. Seaford

ANTIQUES, BRIC-A-BRAC AND JUNK

Possibly due to its proximity to the Continent, East Sussex has become a haven for Auctions, Antique Markets and Shops; a paradise for dealers, collectors and bargain hunters from all over the world. These places are spread throughout the county, although in certain areas, particularly along the coast, they have mushroomed. This gives a wide choice and makes a 'bargain hunting' visit very worth while. So, when clouds are heavy, the rain is threatening to fall and the lure of the countryside is not so strong, try spending a day out foraging into the world of memorabilia. Who knows, for a few pounds you might find something that is worth a fortune. Most indoor Antique Markets are open six days a week from 10.00 a.m. until 5 p.m. and some are open on Sundays too. Shops can be a little more erratic, but should follow normal opening hours.

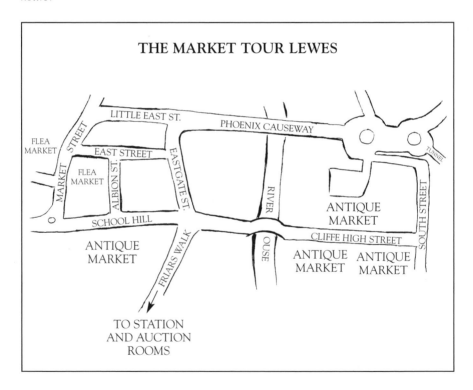

THE MARKET TOUR LEWES

The Market Tour

LEWES (1)

The historical County Town of Lewes is of Saxon origin, has the remains of a Norman castle and some superb examples of Georgian architecture. On the eastern perimeter, on level ground, is The Cliffe, an area with a very different atmosphere.

Here, the beamed and whitewashed properties nudge the River Ouse as it flows by the intriguing complex of Harvey's Brewery under Cliffe Bridge and past restored Victorian warehouses. In Cliffe High Street are three large Antique Markets, vying for business and amongst other things, offering a small but mouth watering selection of Art Nouveau and Art Deco items. One market has two floors of pine for sale, above the 'smalls' at street level. Beyond the markets are several antique shops, stretching past the church. In the opposite direction, half way up School Hill, is yet another market, full of silver, china, jewellery and furniture. At the top of School Hill, turn right into Market Street and halfway down on the right is the Flea Market. Retrace your steps and by the War Memorial, carry on into High Street and there are several more antique shops. It does make one wonder how on earth they all make a living! A final note to earnest bargain hunters. On a Monday morning there is a weekly Antiques/Junk Auction that takes place close to the railway station. The sale starts at 11 a.m. and viewing is prior to this.

HAILSHAM (2)

There are just a couple of antique shops on the A271 before the junction to Hailsham, where you'll find a flea market and numerous charity shops. The market is situated at the southern end of the main street and as this is not generally on the 'traders run' means the occasional 'gem' appears amongst the junk, bric-a-brac or pieces of second-hand furniture.

EASTBOURNE (3)

A handsome Victorian town, well laid out with gardens, a pier, attractions and a wide pleasing seafront, bordering onto the famous cliffs of Beachy Head. East of the main shopping precinct is the part of the town called Seaside. Within a few minutes of each other are two antique markets and some second hand shops, all sited in the Seaside road vicinity. With a bit of searching, it is possible to find a real bargain here. Another antique market can be found in Eastbourne's Old Town, signed from the A22 at Upperton Road.

The Collector's Tour

BEXHILL (4)

The antique/secondhand/junk shops in Bexhill are dotted intermittently between small supermarkets, vegetable shops and any other sort of shop, in a haphazard fashion along the main streets between the sea and the station. Certainly worth a stop to browse for a while and perhaps to visit Bexhill's splendid example of 1930's architecture, The De La Warr pavilion, sited on the attractive promenade. It has a restaurant and teashop overlooking the sea and intermittently, very good antique fairs are held here.

HASTINGS OLD TOWN (5)

Hastings Old Town winds below William the Conqueror's favourite castle on the eastern side of West Hill. The narrow streets, steep steps (in Sussex called 'cat creeps') and lanes (often called 'Twittens') are filled with an unending variety of bric-a-brac and curiosity shops. Searching here is fun. Somehow, this former fishing village with its picturesque features and timbered houses exudes a sense of discovery; a conviction that beneath the dust and cobwebs of yet another low ceilinged premises, there are desirable collectibles, just waiting to be found.

Hastings Old Town.

RYE (6)

One of the loveliest medieval towns in England, Rye sits on a low hill with the River Rother at its foot and the flat secretive Romney Marsh to the east. There is plenty to delight the visitor, for this ancient town that dreams of the past, is full of quaint properties, uneven roof tops, crooked chimneys and cobbled streets. Almost untouched by the present, its atmosphere is that of bygone years and many of the antique shops situated in and around the old timbered warehouses at Strand Quay, have a Dickensian aura. Other antique shops are scattered and one chances upon them by accident when exploring Rye. They are tucked on street corners or tiny squares and one feels almost compelled to purchase something from them, simply to be able to say, "Yes it's lovely isn't it. I found that when we were in Rye."

Strand Quay, Rye.

The Dealer's Tour

BRIGHTON (7)

Once a fishing village called Brighthelmstone, then popularized when the Prince Regent purchased a farmhouse here. He had it rebuilt on a flamboyant scale and slowly it grew into the Royal Pavilion we see today; so Regency Brighton was born; now a large, busy cosmopolitan town. It has also attracted the reputation of being full of antique dealers, both buying and selling. One renowned stretch is The Lanes. Famous for antique jewellery shops, this maze of walkways is only a stone's throw from the Royal Pavilion. The selection of costly and not so costly trinkets is vast, pleasantly confusing and it can be a lesson to eavesdrop on the London dealers bartering and buying here. Prices vary enormously and one could easily while away a day simply browsing, listening and watching the world go by from one of the many cafes. Don't forget to explore the less known "North Laines", situated between North Road and Trafalgar Street. The network of narrow roadways are inhabited with antique shops selling every conceivable form of furniture, bric-a-brac and sheer junk. On Saturday morning there is an excellent antique street market from 7 a.m. to 1 p.m. It's sited in Upper Gardner Street, off North Road. You need to be there early otherwise the bargains will have been snapped up.

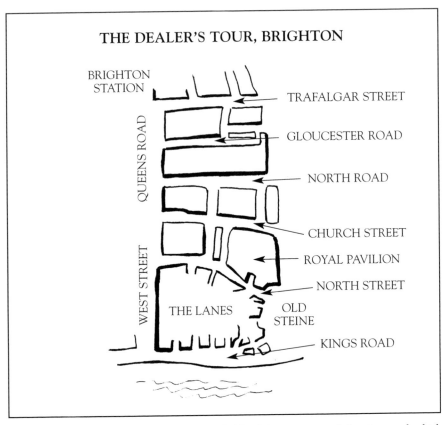

THE DEALER'S TOUR, BRIGHTON

BRIGHTON STATION

TRAFALGAR STREET

GLOUCESTER ROAD

QUEENS ROAD

NORTH ROAD

CHURCH STREET

ROYAL PAVILION

WEST STREET

NORTH STREET

THE LANES

OLD STEINE

KINGS ROAD

On the journey to Seaford, when you reach Newhaven, go round the ring road which encircles the town centre, follow the road back to Brighton and half way up the hill, opposite the entrance to the car park is the Newhaven Flea Market.

SEAFORD (8)

A windswept Victorian town, buffeted by gales and rough seas, that caused considerable damage to the seafront buildings, many of which have now disappeared. In the eighties, the much needed sea wall was built, giving a respite to Seaford and the 'pockets of the past' that remained. The High Street, at the end of the main shopping street, is one such pocket and it is difficult to imagine that less than one hundred years ago, the sea could reach here with alarming regularity. Today, a number of antique and secondhand shops have sprung up in this locality, some of them showing old pictures and postcards of Seaford in flood. Apart from a market on two floors dealing mainly in secondhand books, none of the other shops specialize in anything particular; but the goods on sale include furniture, pictures, china and collectibles. They must be fairly cheap too, judging by the number of dealers that frequent the area.

CRAFTS AND CRAFTSMEN

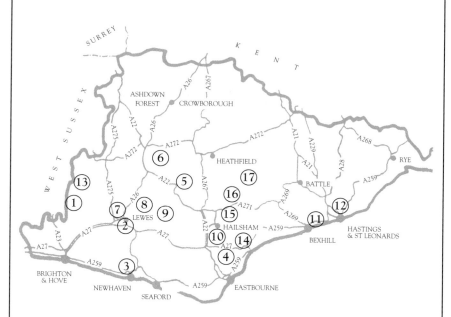

EAST SUSSEX

THE POTTERY TOUR
1. The Craftsmen Gallery - Ditchling
2. Star Brewery - Lewes
3. South Heighton Pottery - near Newhaven
4. J.C.J. Pottery - Stone Cross
5. Pear Tree Pottery - East Hoathly
6. Sharlands Farm Pottery - Blackboys

THE TEXTILE TOUR
7. The Old Needlemakers - Lewes
8. Handweaving - Ringmer
9. The Mohair Centre - Chiddingly
10. Old Loom Mill - Hailsham
11. Patchwork Quilting - St Leonards on Sea
12. Shirley Leaf and Petal Company - Hastings

... AND A WOOD AND METAL TOUR
13. Turner Dumbrell Workshops - Ditchling
14. Glynleigh Studio - Pevensey
15. Thomas Smith Trugs - Herstmonceux
16. Touchwood Pine - Herstmonceux
17. Handmade Furniture - Cowbeech

CRAFTS AND CRAFTSMEN

Historically, crafts in Sussex go back many hundreds of years; back beyond those 17th century ironworks, the medieval potteries of Rye, or the rich jewellery of the Roman era. Probably, to find the beginnings, one would have to go back to the Neolithic flint industry of Cissbury and other downland sites

Today, the word 'craft' appears to have lost its true identity. No longer does it necessarily indicate something created and fashioned by a skilled person; but basket upon basket of mass produced items, given the 'rustic look' and imported from some far-eastern country.

This theme steers clear of any such thing and concentrates on high quality goods, produced by local Sussex craftsmen, in their own studios or working craft centres. Some of these places offer courses or hourly tuition in their given subject, so you could actually learn one or two of the skills yourself. A few of the artisans mentioned in the routes are members of " The Guild of Sussex Craftsmen ", an organization that has been in existence for twenty-five years and holds regular exhibitions. For those who would like more information about the Guild, events or membership, contact the Secretary, Basil Hall on (01342) 810591.

Rye, which is still famous for pottery, is not included in any of the following routes. This is simply because Rye Tourist Information Centre produces an excellent Town Map and leaflets on the local potteries.

The Pottery Tour

THE CRAFTSMEN GALLERY, DITCHLING (1)

In the workshop behind this charming gallery, you can watch Jill Pryke at work on her 'pots'. Jill trained at Wimbledon School of Art and for some years taught pottery to children and adults. She has worked at Ditchling for longer than she cares to remember. Her earthenware pottery is characterized by the gentlest of green or blue glazes and because her technique of decoration allows precise lines, she is able to undertake commissions for personalized presents, anniversary or presentation pieces. The Gallery, which is open shop hours, is easy to find, being slightly north of the crossroads at Ditchling. Also on display are a collection of other crafts and gifts made by local Sussex craftsmen. Tel - (01273) 845246.

STAR BREWERY, FISHER STREET, LEWES (2)

The Old Brewery, which lies close to the High Street, has been skilfully converted to craft workshops and has some of the finest crafts people in Lewes working and selling there. The first stop was the chaotic studio filled with highly decorated pottery by Mo Hamid. Watching him 'throw' his pots is a fascinating business. He trained at West Surrey College of Art and his work has been influenced by Islamic art, Continental Majolica and Dutch Delftware. His hand thrown domestic stoneware would surely make a welcome addition to any kitchen dresser. Mo

Hamid's workshop is open Monday to Saturday, 11 a.m. to 5 p.m. and the telephone number is (01273) 483295.

The Star Brewery is a rambling building and inadvertently, I covered the same area twice, from a different direction, passing on the way, wood turning, bookbinding, glass-blowing and a gallery. The glass-blowing made a particularly interesting stop; to me it always seems such an impossibly delicate procedure, fraught with anxiety lest the whole thing should fold up into a molten ball. The general designs on display seem to have a suggestion of the Art Nouveau style with the merest hint of colour blended (or is it blown) into the glass.

Star Brewery, Fisher Street, Lewes.

SOUTH HEIGHTON POTTERY, NEAR NEWHAVEN (3)

On the A26, north east of Newhaven, well positioned signs indicate the pottery at South Heighton. Situated in an L-shaped section of higgledy-piggledy farm buildings, you will find Chris Lewis and his counterpart, Ursula Mommens, who established the pottery in the 1950's. Together, they produce stoneware in the warmest of terracotta and umber hues with a strong ethnic influence in both shape and decoration. In the 1970's, Chris Lewis spent some time in West Africa studying traditional pottery making and this has influenced many of his designs. In 1980, he built one of the few wood-fired, two chambered kilns in this country, which produces an

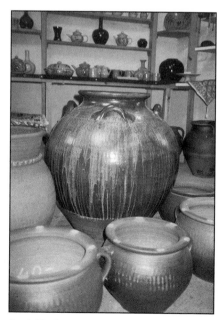

South Heighton Pottery, near Newhaven.

unusual finish on both glazed and unglazed pottery. The studio is open from Monday to Friday and most weekends. Confirmation can be obtained by phoning (01273)514330.

J.C.J. POTTERY, PEELINGS MANOR BARNS, STONE CROSS (4)

The JCJ Pottery workshop is situated amongst some well restored barns at Stone Cross. And don't worry, there is adequate signage from the A27, so getting lost is an impossibility.

Jonathan Chiswell Jones has been making pottery since 1974. He studied at Farnham Art School and Appin Pottery in Scotland. Inspired by Bernard Leach, he then followed his ideal of being self-supporting by making pottery for everyday use. Apart from the usual range of domestic ware in vibrant colours there are crocks, pedestal fruit bowls, oven dishes, lampshades, mirrors, tiles, light pulls and candlesticks. JCJ will also undertake special commissions and commemorative work. Today, Jonathan Chiswells Jones' finely decorated pottery, made in porcelain, can be found in homes throughout the world. The showroom is open all year from 10a.m. to 5p.m. Monday to Saturday. (01323) 469009.

PEARTREE POTTERY, EAST HOATHLY (5)

East Hoathly is bypassed by the A22 Eastbourne road, midway between Uckfield and Hailsham. The pottery is right in the centre of the village, at present in the 'Old Chapel', but about to move to the 'Old Garage', in the village works complex, almost opposite. All the pottery, in several differing patterns, is of stoneware and slip ware: slip ware being earthenware decorated with a fine slip of clay over a different coloured base; and stoneware being a ceramic that falls somewhere between earthenware and porcelain.

Please note: Whilst awaiting Peartree Pottery to be re-established, the Old Chapel has become an Antiques Centre. Do have a look at some of their marvellous examples of old faience (tin glazed earthenware) pottery.

SHARLANDS FARM POTTERY, BLACKBOYS (6)

Less than a mile east of Blackboys, on the B2192 road to Heathfield, is Sharlands Farm. It's situated down a particularly narrow country lane and the turning is very sudden. However, there are one or two faded 'Pottery' signs prior to the turning, so you do get a little bit of warning. A rather lovely complex of barns, behind Sharlands Farm, have been restored to house a pottery, a dried flower shop and a couple of other studios that have always been closed when I've been there. Matthew Bayman has been a full time potter for the last ten years and he is entirely self taught. His pots and tableware are not highly decorated, but beautifully simplistic in varying autumnal hues with the most ingenious twists and curves incorporated into the basic designs. Pottery classes, taken by Matthew, are held at Sharlands Farm and the pottery is open most days, but do check first on; (01435) 862652.

The Textile Tour

THE OLD NEEDLEMAKERS, MARKET STREET, LEWES (7)

This early 19th century candle factory, a stone's throw from the War Memorial, has been sympathetically restored to house an intricate selection of craft shops. Broads candle factory was built around 1820 and closed just short of a hundred years later. Subsequently it became a surgical needle factory, a potter's storeroom and a builder's yard. When demolition threatened the building in the 1970's, conservationists successfully fought to preserve this important piece of local heritage. Even the tall factory chimney remains, providing a distinctive landmark. The needlemaker's craft shops, where the goods are both made and sold, include a selection of adults and children's clothes, patchwork, tapestry, dried flowers, cards and candles. The aroma of coffee and home cooking from the integral brick floored cafe will make an irresistible stop.

HAND WEAVING, RINGMER (8)

Elizabeth Clifford weaves the most magical and subtly coloured lengths of fabric in a mix of wool, silk and cashmere. They are a positive joy to touch and wear. Many of the fabrics have an undulating warp-ways pattern resulting from tie-dyeing the warp prior to weaving. The woven cloth is simply sold in lengths or alternatively, they are made up by Elizabeth, into scarves, shawls and clothes. Elizabeth lives near the Village Green in Ringmer and is open by appointment only on the following number; (01273) 812588.

THE MOHAIR CENTRE, LAUGHTON ROAD, CHIDDINGLY (9)

The Mohair Centre at Brickfield Farm, lies beyond a muddy farm track, by the A22 at Chiddingly. The owners, who had just three Angora goats ten years ago, now farm over a hundred of these appealing, curly animals which produce 600 kgs. of pure mohair each year. In the barn, a shop and spinning room have been established with a selection of hand knits and knit kits, all in beautifully soft kid mohair, on sale.

The goats are sheared twice a year and visitors are welcome to see them at any time, but do wear stout shoes or boots. The mohair which is sold by the gram or the whole fleece straight from the goat, is very different from the commercially produced mohair that has other, synthetic fibres added. For the spinner the mohair can be bought carded or as combed top, natural or dyed and for the knitter, there is hand spun yarn in single or two ply, as well as machine spun yarn in four ply or double knit. The Centre is open daily from 10.00 a.m. until 5.00 p.m. and offers spinning, weaving, dyeing and felt making lessons, plus an adopt-a-goat scheme, where you get first choice on the fleece.

Angora goats, the Mohair Centre, Chiddingly.

The Mohair Centre, Chiddingly.

OLD LOOM MILL, ERSHAM ROAD, HAILSHAM (10)

The Old Loom Mill, a craft and textile centre, is located in the countryside, six miles north of Eastbourne on the B2104 road to Hailsham. It must be paradise for the needle woman, knitter or designer; for on sale are over two tons of fabric lengths and remnants for furnishing and dressmaking at very competitive prices. The mill also carries an enormous range of brightly coloured knitting yarns. These, plus the small crafts section, make it a veritable Aladdin's Cave and it includes a very pleasant coffee shop too.

The Flint Barn Guild of Textile Craftsmen and Artists regularly exhibit and demonstrate their work at the Mill. It provides an excellent opportunity to watch weavers, quilters, spinners and other textile-related crafts in operation. Courses and workshops on silk screen printing, embroidery, patchwork and many more, are held throughout the year.

PATCHWORK QUILTING, ST. LEONARDS-ON-SEA (11)

Louise Bell has been quilt making for fourteen years and draws on a long tradition of quilt making from her own family in Canada. She usually works with American block designs in patterned Liberty fabrics. Louise, who also makes cushions, bags and jackets, lives in St. Leonards and a visit to her patchwork studio is by appointment only on: (01424) 435216.

SHIRLEY LEAF AND PETAL COMPANY, HASTINGS (12)

Don't pass by this unusual working flower and leaf makers Museum. It's situated on the High Street of Hastings Old Town, in the basement of a tiny shop filled with silk flowers. The workshop, ancient machinery and the museum are one. Here, there are more than 10,000 intricately patterned flower and leaf tools of the trade; all over a hundred years old and still in use. So be prepared; for when you step 'below stairs', you will be stepping into a time warp, where the work in progress will be identical to that of a century ago. The only thing that has changed are the customers. In Victorian and Edwardian times, flowers and leaves of velvets, silks and satins were created into hair wreaths, hat decorations, flower collages for dresses and waxed orange blossoms for bridal wear. Violets in every shade were ordered by Woolworths to accompany their 'Devon Violets' perfume.

Today, the Shirley Leaf and Petal Company supplies the television, theatre and film world with flowers and leaves this includes Glyndebourne and The Royal Shakespeare Company. There is a small charge to visit the Museum and should you wish to check opening times, the telephone number is (01424) 427793.

.... And A Wood and Metal Tour

TURNER DUMBRELL WORKSHOPS, DITCHLING (13)

Imaginatively converted barns surrounding a courtyard, make up the Turner Dumbrell Workshops. They lie half a mile north of Ditchling Village on the B2112 road to

Burgess Hill. The greater part of the complex is taken up by Anton Pruden, Silversmith, whose grandfather, also a well known silversmith, became a member of the Guild of St. Joseph and St. Dominic at Ditchling Common. Anton's partner, Rebecca Smith, is a jeweller and between them, they have filled their showroom, next to the workshop, with beautifully crafted objets d'art and jewellery, in both gold and silver.

Also resident at the workshops is Angelo Giovino, who produces fine, individually designed hardwood furniture, and Kevin Hutson, a wood turner; Kevin has been a wood turner for twenty-three years and specializes in exotic bowls and boxes in unusually grained wood. The workshops are open Tuesday to Saturday and the telephone number is (01273) 846338.

THE GLYNLEIGH STUDIO, PEELINGS LANE. PEVENSEY (14)

Skilled Coppersmith, Sam Farnaroff, has a studio near Pevensey Castle, resembling a Blacksmith's shop. The only thing missing is a horse. The disorder, atmospheric cobwebs and smell of metal is remarkably similar to a smithy. But here the similarity ends, for instead of hot iron horseshoes, Sam creates the most wonderfully designed items in copper or brass and occasionally, a pleasing mix of both. The swirls and undulating curves are reminiscent of Art Nouveau and the bowls, vases, trays and candlesticks he crafts must surely be tomorrow's antiques. Before visiting it is advisable to telephone on, (01323) 763456.

THOMAS SMITH TRUGS, HERSTMONCEUX (15)

A trug is a substantial, slatted basket which comes in a variety of sizes (from huge to titchy) and has been traditionally made in Sussex for the last two hundred years. The word 'trug' is derived from the Anglo Saxon word 'trog', meaning boat shaped. Nowadays, some of the baskets have a pretty coloured edging but they are still hand made in the workshop next door, using locally coppiced wood. The Trug Shop is located on the A271 road, in Herstmonceux and is open shop hours.

Thomas Smith Trugs, Herstmonceux.

TOUCHWOOD PINE, HERSTMONCEUX (16)

Ask for Mervyn (I never did find out his surname) at Touchwood Pine, an attractive shop-cum-workshop, stuffed with handmade pine furniture in various stages of completion. Mervyn owns the place and will design anything, for a fee of course, from fitted kitchens to free-standing wardrobes, to antiqued dressers or modern coffee tables. You name it and he'll either have it on sale or make it; just so long as it's in pine. Touchwood is situated in the centre of Herstmonceux on the A271 road and follows shop hours.

Touchwood Pine, Herstmonceux.

HANDMADE FURNITURE, COWBEECH (17)

A visit to Richard Reading's workshop is only for those who are interested in a one off, truly exquisite piece of handmade furniture, with a matching price ticket. Finding the workshop is a task in itself. It's set in the heart of the countryside about three quarters of a mile down Trolliloes Lane, from the 'Merry Harriers' at Cowbeech and is housed in some unrecognizably converted cow sheds, which even the cows must have had difficulty in finding. Richard, who works mainly on commissions, has had his own business making fine furniture for the last twelve years. He tends to use solid hardwoods, often combining many types to form intricate designs. The showroom area within the cow sheds, usually displays some beautiful occasional tables, small bookcases and jewellery boxes. Telephone before visiting on: (01435) 830249.

Handmade furniture, Cowbeech.

FOOD AND WINE

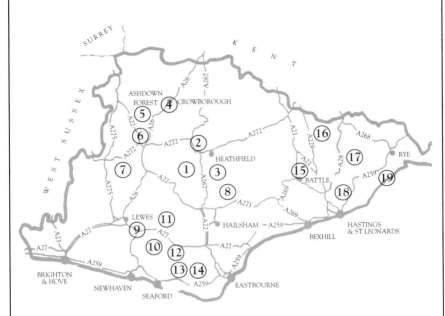

EAST SUSSEX

THE CONNOISSEUR TOUR
1. Merrydown - Horam
2. Forge Cook Shop - Heathfield
3. Star Inn - Old Heathfield
4. Barnsgate Manor Vineyard
5. Duddleswell Tearooms
6. Putlands Farm Shop
7. Old Spot Farm Shop - Piltdown

THE GOURMET TOUR
8. The Sundial - Herstmonceux
9. Riverside - Lewes
10. The Ram - Firle
11. Middle Farm Shop - Firle
12. The English Wine Centre - Alfriston
13. Litlington Tea Gardens - Litlington
14. The Hungry Monk - Jevington

THE WINE TOUR
15. Leeford Vineyards - Whatlington
16. Sedlescombe Organic Vineyards
17. The Rainbow Trout - Broad Oak
18. Carr Taylor Vineyards - Westfield
19. The Tea Tree - Winchelsea

FOOD AND WINE

For all those who want to sample or buy the best of Sussex food and wine, with a little background knowledge, whilst still enjoying a pleasurable day out. The recommended refreshment stops are excellent and the cuisine served is all 'home cooked'.

The "Connoisseur" Tour visits a mixture of outlets whose products fall into the category of 'specialist'. The "Gourmet" Tour concentrates mainly on quality food, locally produced. The "Wine" Tour gives an insight into four vineyards, including an organic one. Interestingly, vine growing, introduced by the Romans, was extensive until the early Middle Ages. It then died out due to climatic changes and cheap imports. Vineyards were re-established here after the Second World War.

The Connoisseur Tour

MERRYDOWN, HORAM (1)

Merrydown, synonymous with cider, has been a household name for the last fifty years. The business, which sprang from a hobby, became established in 1946 by two long standing friends, Jack Ward and Ian Howie. Together with John Kelland-Knight, Merrydown cider and wine was launched on the road to success, one dull November day. The title 'Merrydown' was taken from the house of the same name, owned by Jack Ward and where in fact, the first 400 gallons of vintage cider were produced. Sadly, the two founder members have not lived to see Merrydown's 50th birthday. They both, somewhat curiously, died within four months of each other, in 1986.

A visit to Horam Manor, the home of Merrydown, is an interesting one. There is an audio visual on Merrydown to watch, a huge 19th century horse drawn press to look at, cider tasting to experience and a bottle of something to deliberate upon. The off-licence, adjacent to the works, carries a selection of wines from all four corners of the globe, as well as Merrydown's own products including, of course, their cider, a delightfully old fashioned mead and the new alcoholic lemonade, Two Dogs.

THE FORGE COOKSHOP, HEATHFIELD (2)

Sited in the old railway station, in central Heathfield, the Forge Cookshop shares its name with an elder sibling by ten years, whose premises at Hailsham are actually within an old forge. This second kitchen shop, opened last year, has everything for the cook, from a streamlined garlic crusher to a farmhouse Aga; the only thing missing is the smell of baking. The array of pots, pans, colourful cookware and up to date innovative gadgets festooning the old station walls, will ensure an informative insight into 'what's new' in the world of catering.

Forge Cookshop, Heathfield.

THE STAR INN, OLD HEATHFIELD (3)

An unspoilt rural hamlet, not to be confused with the commercial town of the same name. The old church, much of it rebuilt in the early 19 century, towers above the ancient Star Inn, whose low beamed interior and attractively terraced gardens are a fitting introduction to the delicious food that is served on the premises. It's obviously gourmet patronage keep the owners busy. The menu offers tempting cuisine such as: wild rabbit with juniper berries and wine; local pheasant with herbs; smoked fish platter and scrambled eggs. For the less adventurous, there is fresh Hastings cod and chips or steak and kidney pie. And for those who like something a little lighter at lunch time, there is a meat or fish pate with slivers of warm baked bread. Puds, which command a menu board all to themselves, are totally gluttonous. Try one, if you can.

The Star Inn, Old Heathfield.

BARNSGATE MANOR VINEYARD, HERONS GHYLL (4)

One of the most beautiful vineyards in Britain, with panoramic views across the Weald to the South Downs. Barnsgate, a fifty four acre farm with ten acres of vines, is located on the A26 at Herons Ghyll, four miles north of Uckfield. It is open daily throughout the year, although the self-guided vineyard trail becomes a bit muddy in mid winter. The vineyard, first planted in 1970, now produces about 14,000 bottles of wine each year and recently, a sparkling champagne-type wine had been added to the list. The tasting and purchase of wine is done at the vineyard shop. So, whilst the adults are concentrating on the epicurean side of life, the children can wander off to watch the llamas, donkeys and black Wenslydale sheep that graze in the surrounding pastures. There is a restaurant, tearoom and a large patio, all benefiting from the magnificent views.

DUDDLESWELL TEAROOMS, DUDDLESWELL (5)

A popular tearoom, set back from the B2026 road in Ashdown Forest. Oddly enough, the 'olde worlde' exterior belies an almost cafe-like interior. Nevertheless, the all time British favourite of freshly baked scones, jam and cream, washed down with a substantial pot of tea, make it a recommendable four o'clock break.

PUTLANDS FARM SHOP, DUDDLESWELL (6)

Indicated from the B2026 road, in the heart of Ashdown Forest, this tiny farm shop lies at the end of a muddy, rutted track, doubling as a public footpath. The owners of the farm hope to negotiate an alternative entrance in the near future.

Putlands Farm concentrates on products made from locally supplied sheep's milk, where the ewes have been grazed and any feed is free from animal protein, antibiotics and hormones. In the farm shop, which is no more than an overgrown shed, you will find on sale: sheep's milk and yoghurts, both fruit and natural, fromage frais and a selection of sheep's cheeses. There is, a medium soft fat cheese with herbs, Ricotta, a hard cheese called 'Duddleswell' and Halloumi, a traditional Mediterranean cheese, which is very versatile. Do try this one as a 'nibble'. Simply slice the Halloumi into rounds about half an inch thick, then 'dry fry' on both sides until lightly brown. Top with a portion of cherry tomato and serve. The shop is open most days, but it is advisable to telephone first on (01825) 712647. (see title page).

OLD SPOT FARM SHOP, PILTDOWN (7)

Situated on the A272, just west of Piltdown, is Old Spot Farm Shop; a large chalet type building, well signed with ample parking and carrying a good range of Sussex produce. However, the main speciality here is additive free meat. It is all reared on Sussex farms, without the use of antibiotics or growth promoters. So much more acceptable than the supermarket equivalent but, of course, more expensive. The sausages come in twenty different varieties and contain no colour or preservative.

The bacons and hams are superb and apart from meat, local poultry and game are available (the latter when in season). The owners, Roger and Diane Gould, are usually around to answer queries and also have an impressive brochure containing information and the cost of all their meats. The shop is open every day except Monday, but if you wish to check opening times, telephone (01825) 723929

The Gourmet Tour

THE SUNDIAL, HERSTMONCEUX (8)

It seemed like a good idea to make the Gourmet Tour a little flexible by beginning and ending with two East Sussex restaurants of long standing repute. Therefore, should you choose to do this jaunt in reverse, you can be sure of ending the day in a relaxed atmosphere with gourmet food and a glass of recommended wine. The Sundial at Gardner Street, Herstmonceux has been in business for many years and claims to have customers who travel from afar to enjoy the chef's culinary skills - served in the softly lit, low ceilinged dining area. Just one word of advice, book first. (01323) 832217.

RIVERSIDE, CLIFF HIGH STREET. LEWES (9)

Adjacent to Cliffe Bridge, their foundations nudged by the River Ouse, are several Victorian warehouses in various stages of conversion to shops, offices and homes. Riverside, now completed, offers culinary buying and eating under one cavernous white painted roof. It is reminiscent of a French market, the noise, the discerning buying and somewhere, the bitter aroma of coffee hanging in the air. On the ground floor is an additive free meat counter. Alongside is the Deli counter, with smoked hams, bacon and salamis. The fish counter bulges with fish, fresh and pink from Newhaven and opposite with a window overlooking the river, you'll find 'Say Cheese'. Here, the enormous counter is filled with a variety of cheeses from around the world and include a good selection of Sussex cheeses. Why not taste these local ones first? There is Burndell, a full fat pressed goat's cheese in yellow wax, from an organic farm in West Sussex; the smoked version is good too. How about Shere Devilment, a garlicky cheese finished with black pepper; or Chancton, a soft creamy with a mould ripened crust, or even a subtle blue cheese, called Chalk Hill Blue (presumably after the butterfly). Complementary to this lot there's home baked bread, butter croissants, Sussex biscuits, olives and sun dried tomatoes, as well as local apple juice and cider. Fine wines, health foods and a cafe-cum-bar all jostle for space downstairs at Riverside. Upstairs is mostly given over to a French type brasserie with uncluttered tables and peaceful views.

THE RAM, FIRLE (10)

The winding lane leading from the A27 near Lewes into this unspoilt village, culminates under the escarpment of Firle Beacon. During the 18th century, there were four public houses in Firle; The Polecat, The Ram, The Woolpack and on the old turnpike road at the foot of the downs, The Beanstalk. Now only The Ram remains, a 17th century flint and tiled coaching inn. Its appearance is somewhat shabby and basic, bare wooden floors, yellowed paint, a jumble of tables and chairs: perhaps that's a part of its charm. It doesn't need those glitzy trappings. It has a reputation for a good atmosphere, excellent traditional food and is Egon Ronay recommended several times over. The hot favourite (not to make a pun of it) seems to be 'Sausage Rumblethumps'. This consists of a baked mash of potato, onion, red cabbage and cheese, topped with a couple of sausages. The sea food pie was also popular and vegetarians were catered for with 'Leek and Pepper Frittata'. The Ram's Ploughmans are not cheap, but they are the best you'll ever get, with several choices of farmhouse cheeses, home baked hams and pates, all served with granary bread. The desert menu had some rib-sticking titles on it, like Baked Jam Roly Poly, Fruit Pie, Bakewell Tart and one entitled 'Icky Sticky Pudding'. I never did find out what it was.

Highly recommended is a visit to Firle Place, home of the Gage family for centuries. Open during the season, it contains a superb collection of furniture and works of art set in extensive grounds. Its restaurant is well known for its Sussex Cream Teas and excellent home cooking. Admission charge.

Crafts at Middle Farm Shop, Firle.

MIDDLE FARM SHOP, FIRLE (11)

Middle Farm is located on the A27 road soon after the turning to Firle. It could be dubbed the 'Supermarket' of Farm Shops, owing to its size and many sections. In the long main barn there is a butcher's where you can purchase fresh or frozen, additive-free meat. In the kitchen section is a farmhouse bakery, next to that is a dairy, then a fresh fruit and veg section. Whole foods take up a good deal of space along with a host of other goodies, such as jams and pickles. Another barn houses the English farm cider centre, where over a 150 English ciders are available, either bottled or draught, including the farm 'scrumpy cider'. Yet a further barn in this courtyard complex is a tearoom. Finally, in solitary state nearby, is an ivy covered barn divided into a couple of very good craft workshops. One specializes in caning and rush seating, (now you know where to get that chair repaired), the other in spinning and weaving, with a small area of hand knits for sale. Oh, and by the way, there's a garden section too. Middle Farm is open all day, every day.

THE ENGLISH WINE CENTRE, ALFRISTON (12)

A range of low barns at the head of the Cuckmere Valley, comprise The English Wine Centre which has now been established for more than twenty years. This is where quality English wines come together with the regional food banner, 'A Taste of Sussex', in perfect harmony. English wines and a selection of the 'Taste of Sussex' products, sold in small shops throughout the county, are always on sale at the

English Wine Centre, Alfriston.

Centre. Wine tastings usually take place in the Wine Museum, a building with a particularly rustic aura, sporting artefacts, displays and information on wine production since Roman times. The only thing lacking is a Roman slave treading grapes. The Wine Centre is open daily throughout the year.

LITLINGTON TEA GARDENS, LITLINGTON (13)

Litlington lies about two miles south of the A27 near Polegate. The only indication of a tea garden in the village, is some rather scruffy parking (shared with the adjacent nursery), a sign and some steps; otherwise it's hidden from view by trees and flowering shrubs. A pathway snakes through the shrubbery finishing at a wide sunny lawn with chairs and tables positioned in arbours or summerhouses. A single storey structure houses an indoor tea room and the kitchen. It's all very Edwardian and the teas themselves echo of that long gone era: hot floury scones, wafer thin sandwiches, light jammy sponges and the heavier cousin, rich fruit cake. Don't miss this glorious feast. The tea garden is open during the season and also serves lunches at weekends.

THE HUNGRY MONK, JEVINGTON (14)

A discreet and charming downland village, 'twixt Polegate and the sea. The Hungry Monk restaurant, renowned for many years for its superb food and matching atmosphere, was once the home of the unscrupulous smuggler, Jevington Jig. Therefore, you would be forgiven for thinking the exterior commemorative plaque relates to him. But look at it carefully, instead it reads "Banoffi Pie, born here, 1972". For those who are not familiar with the famous Banoffi concoction, this is what it consists of:- One cooked pastry case filled with sliced banana and a large can of condensed milk, previously boiled in the can for two or three hours, poured over it. The consistency of the milk is thick, scrummy toffee, but the boiling bit is rather tricky. I make my own, not so good version. After that, cover the pie with cream and serve. It has to be the best pud around.

The Wine Tour

LEEFORD VINEYARDS, WHATLINGTON (15)

Leeford lies in undulating, south facing countryside between Battle and the A21. This exceptionally pretty vineyard, established in 1982, must surely dispel the myth that vines only look comfortable growing on the sun baked terraces of Provence. The seven varieties of vines, grown in Leeford's fifty acres, look very comfortable and attractive indeed. The grapes from these vines are often blended in the wine making; such as Pinot Noir and Zweigeltrebre, which together make Saxon Rose, a medium dry Rose wine with a strawberry aroma. Saxon Crown is a light, fresh dry white wine; a blend of the grapes from the Reichensteiner, Huxelrebe and Kerner

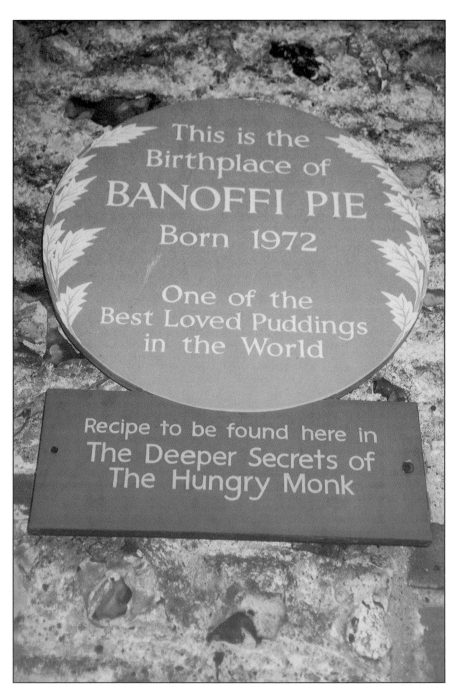

The Hungry Monk, Jevington

vines. The vineyard shop, where one can taste all these bewildering varieties, is sited in one of a pair of Victorian oast houses; a reminder that this land was once used for growing hops and the oasts for drying. A large new winery has just been completed and wine tours can be organized by appointment. Leeford Vineyards are open daily from Easter to Christmas and weekdays only from January to Easter.

SEDLESCOMBE ORGANIC VINEYARD, CRIPPS CORNER (16)

Sedlescombe Organic Vineyard is tucked in a valley on the B2244 between Sedlescombe and Cripps Corner. Set amongst trees, the vineyard shop and rustic winery feature an unusual 1912 cast iron and oak grape press, actually used until 1991. There is also information on natural wine making and a selection of organic wines on sale. Several detailed nature trails, meander through the vineyards and woodland where you might, if you're lucky, catch a glimpse of the resident woodpeckers. This is also a very pleasant spot for a picnic .... with a bottle of wine. The vineyard is open daily from April to December and from January to March, weekend afternoons only.

THE RAINBOW TROUT, BROAD OAK (17)

With a name like The Rainbow Trout, there are no prizes for guessing what the speciality is at this highly recommended and very pleasant lunch-time pub. Although fishy dishes take up the greater part of the menu, there is a good choice for non fish lovers, which includes home made steak and kidney pud. For a light snack, there is sausages, ploughmans, or crusty salad rolls filled with smoked salmon, prawns or pate. If you're seriously into fish, how about a hot or cold lobster or Mediterranean prawns with garlic, fresh Dover sole cooked in butter and lemon or grilled trout stuffed with prawns and asparagus, accompanied by a glass of wine, (French perhaps this time!) Vegetarians are well catered for and so too, wait for it ..... are dogs, a few biscuits and water supplied. What more could you ask for?

CARR TAYLOR VINEYARDS, WESTFIELD (18)

A meticulous and successful vineyard of 37 acres, established on an experimental basis in 1971. Commercial planting commenced in 1973 and Carr Taylor pioneered the high trellis system that enables grapes to be produced in quantity, even in poor weather. The types of vines have been carefully chosen to produce a distinctive flavour and these, as you will notice as you walk round the vineyard trails, are grown in blocks. There are organized tours around the large and impressive winery that appears not to be dissimilar to a hospital operating theatre. The grapes, most of which are harvested in October, are crushed into grape juice, then fermented with a cultured wine yeast in the 70 vats housed in the winery. With due care and attention they are ready for bottling the following March. The splendid vineyard

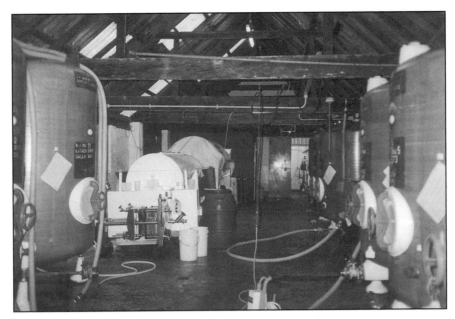

Carr Taylor Vinyards, Westfield.

shop where wine tastings and sales take place, also serve light refreshments. Carr Taylor Vineyards are open daily throughout the year, except for January, when it is closed at weekends.

THE TEA TREE, WINCHELSEA (19)

After a day of tasting wine, what better place to indulge in a sobering cup of tea than Winchelsea. For when Winchelsea was a port, during the 13th and 14th centuries, it became the home of many wealthy wine traders and records suggest there were no less than fifty wine cellars here. (See 'Lost Villages' for further information). The Tea Tree is in the High Street of this historic town and offers coffees, light lunches and traditional teas. All the food is home-made and the cakes are particularly irresistible. There are several variations of the set teas, as well as a cream tea. Freshly ground coffee and loose teas are for sale. The restaurant is open every day except Tuesday and is closed during the month of January.

EAST SUSSEX VINEYARDS
(open to the public)

BARKHAM MANOR
Barkham Manor, Piltdown,
Uckfield TN22 3XE
Tel: (01825) 722103

CARR TAYLOR
Yew Tree Farm, Westfield,
Hastings TN35 4SG
Tel: (01424) 752501

HIDDEN SPRING
Vines Cross Road, Horam,
Nr. Heathfield TN21 0HF
Tel: (01435) 812640

BARNSGATE MANOR
Barnsgate Manor, Heron's
Ghyll, Uckfield TN22 4DB
Tel: (01825) 713366

ENGLISH WINE CENTRE
Drusillas Roundabout,
Alfriston BN26 5QS
Tel: (01323) 870164

LEEFORD
Battle
TN33 0NQ
Tel: (01424) 773183

BREAKY BOTTOM
Rodmell,
Nr. Lewes
Tel: (01273) 476427

FLEXERNE *
Fletching Common,
Newick BN8 4JJ
Tel: (01825) 722548

ST. GEORGES
Waldron,
Nr. Heathfield
Tel: (01435) 812156

* By prior appointment only

PICK AND MIX GEOGRAPHICAL INDEX

EAST SUSSEX

A

B

C

D

TOURIST INFORMATION CENTRES

BATTLE
    88, High Street   Tel: (01424) 773721

BEXHILL
    De La Warr Pavilion   Tel: (01424) 212023

BOSHIP
    Lower Dicker   Tel: (01323) 442667

BRIGHTON
    10, Bartholomew Square   Tel: (01273) 323755

EASTBOURNE
    Cornfield Road   Tel: (01323) 411400

HAILSHAM
    The Library, Western Rd.   Tel: (01323) 844426

HASTINGS
    4, Robertson Terrace   Tel: (01424) 781111

HOVE
    Church Road   Tel: (01273) 778087

LEWES
    187, High Street   Tel: (01273) 483448

PEACEHAVEN
    Meridian Centre   Tel: (01273 582668

PEVENSEY
    Castle Cottage (Easter - Oct)   Tel: (01323) 761444

RYE
    Heritage Centre, Strand Quay   Tel: (01797) 226696

SEAFORD
    Clinton Place   Tel: (01323) 897426